"Love is the most powerful apologetic. It is the essential component in reaching the whole person in a fragmented world. Tullian understands the deep yearnings of this generation and thoughtfully expresses how making a difference as Christians in this world begins with a willingness to engage this world differently."

—RAVI ZACHARIAS, author and speaker

"*Unfashionable* is theologically careful, biblically grounded, and culturally in touch. It will challenge you and point you to the radically Christ-centered life you were saved by God's amazing grace to live. Tullian Tchividjian hits us between the eyes when he says, 'Christians who retreat into a comfortable subculture are bad missionaries—it's that simple.' It *is* that simple, and this book will help you find the way out!"

—DANIEL L. AKIN, president of Southeastern
Baptist Theological Seminary

"With the right balance of reproof and encouragement, critique and construction, *Unfashionable* displays with succinct, vivid, and engaging clarity the relevance of the gospel over the trivialities that dominate our lives and our churches right now. The message of this book is of ultimate importance and its presentation is compelling."

—MICHAEL HORTON, J. Gresham Machen Professor,
Westminster Seminary California, and host
of *White Horse Inn*

"Although the ancient Israelites were called by God to be a 'holy nation,' they failed to reach their world because they were so much like it. Today's church is succumbing to the same error. And this is what makes Tullian Tchividjian's book *Unfashionable* so prophetic and such a book for this day. May the church take note—and reach the world!"

—R. KENT HUGHES, senior pastor emeritus,
College Church in Wheaton, Illinois

"It is not easy to stand athwart the tides of the culture and challenge them without sounding either terribly prissy or hopelessly out of date. How can a thoughtful Christian be genuinely contemporary while never succumbing to the merely faddish and temporary? The challenges are enormous—but they are also tied to the most elementary tenets of Christian faithfulness. Tullian Tchividjian is a helpful and engaging guide through these troubled waters."

—D. A. CARSON, Trinity Evangelical Divinity School
and author of *Christ and Culture Revisited*

"In *Unfashionable,* Tullian calls us to a holistic, gospel-centered journey that invites us, in a fresh way, to be in the world but not of it. He shows us how to be God's peculiar people by displaying his kingdom in the world around us."

—RICK MCKINLEY, founding pastor of Imago Dei
Community and author of *This Beautiful Mess*

"Tullian masterfully articulates the importance of the 'both and,' showing that, in order for Christians to make a profound difference in our world, we must both gain a full understanding of the gospel and express it practically in our world."

—GABE LYONS, founder of Q and coauthor
of *UnChristian*

"Here's what we need: a young, fresh, outspoken voice calling for renewal and reform in kingdom language. With a deep appreciation for the Christian past, a powerful grasp of the gospel, and a voice that resonates with those calling for renewal today, Tullian represents a breed of young church leaders who might just help us navigate our way through the stodginess of tradition and the silliness of much that is emerging as Christianity today. May his tribe increase."

—T. M. MOORE, Wilberforce Forum and author
of *Culture Matters*

"In *Unfashionable,* Tullian Tchividjian offers all of us a window into his own life, full as it is of reading the Word and the world at the same time. His vision is theologically rich and pastorally engaging, calling us to join him in thinking deeply about things that matter most, namely, the reality that faith always shapes vocation, which always shapes culture."

—STEVEN GARBER, the Washington Institute
and author of *The Fabric of Faithfulness*

"Tullian Tchividjian persuasively argues that difference makers must be different. This book is an important and necessary reminder that Christians who strive to be relevant end up being redundant, while those who challenge our culture just may change the world."

—MICHAEL E. WITTMER, professor of systematic theology
at Grand Rapids Theological Seminary and author of
Heaven Is a Place on Earth

"*Unfashionable* gets back to the heart of the kingdom mission and the agenda of the gospel message. Striking a balance between being 'in' but not 'of' the world is not easy. Tullian, however, clearly and convincingly shows the way by telling how we can cultivate a gospel-centered outlook and lifestyle."

—ED STETZER, president of LifeWay Research
and author of *Planting Missional Churches*

"What does it mean to be in the world but not of it? To what degree should we conform to the culture, or how should we differ and why? *Unfashionable* addresses these questions directly and helpfully, pointing the way to faithful discipleship in the twenty-first century."

—LUDER G. WHITLOCK JR., president of Excelsis
and author of *The Spiritual Quest*

"Fashion is but a phase. If Christians want to see lasting change as the kingdom of Jesus Christ expands, they will refuse to seek the world's acclaim. Tullian Tchividjian writes with a pastor's gift for admonition and encouragement as he discerns the church's failures and opportunities to represent Christ in this world."

—COLLIN HANSEN, editor at large of *Christianity Today* and author of *Young, Restless, Reformed*

"As Christians continue to chase relevance like a dog chasing its own tail, the world around us is quietly looking for something more— something deeper, something less self-aware, something unfashionable. With clear, crisp writing, *Unfashionable* challenges us to stop imitating the world and start working to renew her. Tullian makes it once again 'cool' to be uncool."

—KEVIN DEYOUNG, pastor and author of *Why We're Not Emergent*

"The most wonderful thing happened to me as I read *Unfashionable:* I was helped. There are so many books that are interesting and informative, but few end up being practically helpful. *Unfashionable* is one of them. As I read this cogent call for the church to live against the world for the world, I saw several ways that my thinking, affections, and actions needed to be prayerfully addressed. I trust the same will happen with anyone who dares to consider the contents of this book."

—THABITI ANYABWILE, senior pastor, First Baptist Church of Grand Cayman, and author of *What Is a Healthy Church Member?* and *The Faithful Preacher*

"*Unfashionable*—unrelentingly orthodox and winsomely written— is a call to follow Christ in being so biblically different from the world that the world can once again see the attractiveness of the gospel. I hope it becomes fashionable for Christians to read and discuss *Unfashionable*. Reading it made me glad to be a believer."

—DENIS HAACK, editor in chief of *Critique* and founder of Ransom Fellowship

"If you are a Christian who longs to see the gospel shape every area of your life so that you make a difference in this world for the glory of God, you will find *Unfashionable* a remarkable guide. With penetrating insight, Tullian exposes the idolatry of our world and shows how the gospel creates a people who are both for and against the world in a way that makes much of the God who will one day make all things new."

—DAN CRUVER, director of Together for Adoption

"*Unfashionable* helps to show the compelling nature of living unfashionable lives for the sake of God and his kingdom. Not only does Tullian lay out helpful instructions, but he provides biblically grounded foundations for why we are to live such unfashionable lives in our fast-paced, often unreflective lifestyles."

—ALLEN WAKABAYASHI, InterVarsity Christian Fellowship
and author of *Kingdom Come: How Jesus Wants to
Change the World*

"The Tchividjian touch is effective because he doesn't play games on the issue of cultural engagement. Instead, he keeps taking the reader back to Scripture. His diagnosis is soberly biblical. But much more heartening is that his solutions are also so straightforwardly biblical. No bells and whistles here. Just the honest application of God's Word as the most promising pattern for making the church attractive to the world."

—JOEL BELZ, founder of *World* magazine

unfashinable

making a difference in the world
by being different

tullian tchividjian
foreword by **timothy keller**

MULTNOMAH
BOOKS

UNFASHIONABLE
PUBLISHED BY MULTNOMAH BOOKS
12265 Oracle Boulevard, Suite 200
Colorado Springs, Colorado 80921

The names of some individuals whose stories are told in this book have been changed to protect their privacy.

ISBN 978-1-60142-085-5
ISBN 978-1-60142-178-4 (electronic)

Published in the United States by WaterBrook Multnomah, an imprint of The Doubleday Publishing Group, a division of Random House Inc., New York.

MULTNOMAH and its mountain colophon are registered trademarks of Random House Inc.

Library of Congress Cataloging-in-Publication Data
Tchividjian, Tullian.
   Unfashionable : making a difference in the world by being different / Tullian Tchividjian. — 1st ed.
       p. cm.
   Includes bibliographical references and index.
   ISBN 978-1-60142-085-5 — ISBN 978-1-60142-178-4 (electronic)
   1. Christian life. I. Title.
   BV4501.3.T395 2009
   248.4—dc22

                           2008054714

Printed in the United States of America
2009—First Edition

10 9 8 7 6 5 4 3 2 1

SPECIAL SALES
Most WaterBrook Multnomah books are available at special quantity discounts when purchased in bulk by corporations, organizations, and special-interest groups. Custom imprinting or excerpting can also be done to fit special needs. For information, please e-mail SpecialMarkets@WaterBrook Press.com or call 1-800-603-7051.

●●●●●

To Kim
"I cannot live, I can't breathe, unless you do this with me."
(Angels & Airwaves)

The great guide of the world is fashion and its god is respectability—two phantoms at which brave men laugh! How many of you look around on society to know what to do? You watch the general current and then float upon it! You study the popular breeze and shift your sails to suit it. True men do not so! You ask, "Is it fashionable? If it is fashionable, it must be done." Fashion is the law of multitudes, but it is nothing more than the common consent of fools.

— CHARLES SPURGEON

c ntents

Part 4: **The Charge**

freword

Tullian Tchividjian bravely steps into one of the hottest debates in contemporary evangelicalism—the divisive issue of how Christians should relate to our broader culture. He does so with grace, providing us with one of the most accessible guides to this issue that we have.

Let me give a brief outline of the current conflict as I see it.

Traditionally, evangelicals' attitude toward culture has been one of relative indifference. It was thought, after all, that this world is only going to burn up in the end. Only human souls last forever. What matters, then, is to convert as many people as possible, and if we do so during the time we have left here on earth, society will be bettered and changed "one heart at a time." Many churches and Christians still understand things this way. But during the last generation, as American social values changed drastically and as the distinction between Christianity and the rest of the culture has sharpened, many Christians have felt pressured to respond. Three very different approaches have emerged.

First, some perceive the main problem to be the loss of moral absolutes. They insist that Christians have been too passive and must "take the culture back" through politics and grass-roots social activism around issues such as abortion, same-sex marriage, fatherhood, traditional gender roles, and abstinence education. They complain that Christians have become too much like the culture since we have as many divorces and abortions and since many no longer really believe in absolute truth. Young people are therefore encouraged to recover a Christian worldview and then to penetrate the culture and accomplish a conservative version of the "long march through the elite institutions" that the young 1960s radicals achieved over the last thirty years.

In reaction to this approach, other Christians have insisted that the main problem today is the church's irrelevance to the concerns of people and the problems of society. While the first group thinks Christians are too assimilated into the world around them, this second group believes Christians are too withdrawn into their own subculture. Believers speak in language that is now undecipherable to the average person. In particular, they are indifferent to the inequality, injustice, and suffering in the world. In this model the church is called to connect with the felt needs of people and especially to work against inequality and injustice in society. As different as they seem on the surface, older churches like Willow Creek and Saddleback and many emerging churches basically share this way of relating Christ to culture.

The last of the three approaches believes the main problem today is that both the conservative evangelical church and the liberal mainline church have been corrupted by the "Constantinian error" of seeking to reform the world to be like the church. Instead the church has become like the world. It is dominated by the political economy of capitalism and liberal democracy. Trying to change the world seduces Christians into conformity to the world in order to get into positions of influence. Trying to be relevant and to meet felt needs only turns the church into another consumer mall. Instead the church needs to recapture its calling to be an alternative society, a counterculture. It needs to follow Christ "outside the camp," identifying with the poor and marginalized. It needs to have rich, liturgical worship that shapes Christians into a new society. It should stop trying to bring the kingdom of Christ into the world and simply live as signs of the future kingdom. Christians certainly live in the world and have secular vocations, but in them they should aim to act as good citizens and neighbors like anyone else. They shouldn't try to transform the culture.

So who is right? Is the main problem a lack of evangelism? Or is it the failure of Christians to live out their worldview in the cultural institutions? Or is it our inability to connect with nonbelievers in their own language, to work against injustice, hunger, and poverty?

Or is it the thinness and lack of distinctiveness of our own Christian communities?

When one takes a view of these models from thirty thousand feet, it is not too hard to realize why they all have so many adherents. Each one is onto something extremely important. Their biggest weakness, however, is that they tend to define themselves against each other instead of against the world. This means that, for all their strengths and insights, none of them seems to be able to see the strengths in the other approaches. This leads to imbalances and overreaching.

What I love about Tullian's book is that he implicitly critiques all of these approaches, not by directly trying to refute them, but by selecting the strengths of each approach, explaining and illustrating each one in ways easy to grasp, and then showing how at a congregational level they can be woven together into a coherent whole. Here you will learn how we must contextualize, how we Christians should be as active in Hollywood, Wall Street, Greenwich Village, and Harvard Square as in the halls of Washington DC. And yet there are ringing calls to form a distinct, "thick" Christian counterculture as perhaps the ultimate witness to the presence of the future, the coming of the kingdom.

Tullian gives us a great example of how the emphases I've described can be combined in a local church in our own cultural moment. Read it carefully and you will profit greatly.

—Timothy Keller, senior pastor of
Redeemer Presbyterian Church, New York City,
and author of *The Reason for God*

Are You Unfashionable?

THIS IS A SERIOUS BOOK about a topic that Christ followers need to take seriously if they're going to make a serious difference in the world. So I thought it would be fun to begin with something not so serious: a David Letterman–style top ten list that will hopefully, in an uncomfortably fun sort of way, help you understand what I mean by the term *unfashionable*.

You May Be Too Fashionable If...

10. You can look around at church and notice that everybody is basically the same age as you are, and they look and dress pretty much like you do.

9. You think it's very uncool to sing a worship song that was "in" five years ago—much less sing a hymn from another century.

8. It's been a long time since you disagreed with anything said by Oprah.

7. You've attended a "leadership" conference where you learned more about organization and props (structural renovation) than proclamation and prayer (spiritual reformation).

6. Your goal in spending time with non-Christians is to demonstrate that you're really no different than they are, and to prove this you curse like a sailor, drink like a fish, and smoke like a chimney.

5. You've concluded that everything new is better than any-thing old *or* that everything old is better than anything new.

4. You think that the way Jesus lived is more important than what he said—that his deeds are more important than his doctrine.

3. You believe that the best way to change our culture is to elect a certain kind of politician.

2. The church you've chosen is defined more by its reaction to "boring traditional" churches than by its response to a needy world.

1. The one verse you most wish wasn't in the Bible is John 14:6, where Jesus says, "*I* am the way, and the truth, and the life. *No one* comes to the Father except through *me*." That's way too close minded!

Part 1

The Call

A Cry for Difference

One of the great attractions of Christianity to me is
its sheer absurdity.

— MALCOLM MUGGERIDGE

●●●●●●

I WISH EVERYONE could have had my upbringing. I come from a line
of devout Christians who have been used by God in various ways to
change the world. As far back as I can trace, strong Christian convic-
tion and devotion to Jesus Christ have been defining marks of my
family legacy—a gracious gift to me from God, something I neither
asked for nor deserved.

That heritage goes beyond my maternal grandparents, Billy and
Ruth Graham, faithful servants of the kingdom of God for the last
sixty-five years. It also includes my dad, a respected psychologist, who
has always put service to God and others before himself. And it
includes my mom, a Christian writer and speaker whose ministry to
women, especially to mothers and wives, has spanned the globe.

With a large family entrusted to them (I'm the middle of seven
children—five boys and two girls), my parents worked hard to create
a home atmosphere that encouraged us kids to take God seriously but
not take ourselves too seriously. The flavor of Christianity they culti-
vated in our family was joyful, warm, inviting, hospitable, and real, not
legalistic or oppressive.

We laughed hard and often, mostly at ourselves. We were trained
to think deeply about God, to feel passionately for God, and to live

urgently in response to God. The gospel, according to my parents, needed to be understood with our heads, felt with our hearts, and worked out with our hands. Anything short of this was a less-than-balanced expression of true Christianity. They taught us to think, to read, to pray, to sing, to cry, to love, to serve.

Growing up, my brothers and sisters walked the straight and narrow for the most part, rarely giving my parents any real trouble. And then there was me. Different story!

Maybe it was because, despite my healthy upbringing, I found it difficult being the middle child. There's a large age gap between my three older siblings and my three younger ones, and I couldn't figure out if I was the youngest of the older set or the oldest of the younger group. I was in the unenviable position of being both a youngest child and an oldest child. Faced with this tension, I should have "cast all my anxiety on the Lord," as I was taught. But I didn't. Unsure of where I fit inside the family, I set out trying to fit outside of it.

At sixteen I dropped out of high school. Then, because my lifestyle had become so disruptive to the rest of the household, my grieving parents decided to kick me out of the house. But I refused to go quietly. On that memorable, dreadful afternoon, I was escorted off my parents' property by the police.

I'll never forget sitting in the back of that police car and looking out the window at my crying mother. I felt no grief, no shame, no regret. In fact, I was pleased with my achievements. Having successfully freed myself from the constraints of teachers and parents, I could now live every young guy's dream. No one to look over my shoulder, no one to breathe down my neck, no one to tell me what I could and couldn't do. I was finally free—or so I thought.

My newfound freedom had me chasing the things of this world harder than most others my age. I sought acceptance, affection, meaning, and respect behind every worldly tree and under every worldly rock. The siren song of our culture promised me that by pursuing the right people, places, and things, I'd find the belonging I craved. If I

could look, act, and talk a certain way, my deep itch to fit in would finally get scratched.

But it didn't work out that way. The more I pursued those things, the more lost I felt. The more I drank from the well of worldly acceptance, the thirstier I became; the faster I ran toward godless pleasure, the farther I felt from true fulfillment; the more I pursued freedom, the more enslaved I became. At twenty-one I found myself hungering for belonging more than ever.

The world hadn't satisfied me the way it had promised, the way I'd anticipated. The world's message and methods had, in fact, hung me out to dry. I felt betrayed. Lied to. I desperately needed to be rescued by something—or Someone—out of this world.

Punctured Roof

One morning I woke up with an aching head and a sudden stark awareness of my empty heart. Having returned to my apartment after another night of hard partying on Miami's South Beach, I'd passed out with all my clothes on. Hours later, as I stirred to a vacant, painful alertness, I realized it was Sunday morning. I was so broken and longing for something transcendent, for something higher than anything this world has to offer, that I decided to go to church. I didn't even change my clothes. I jumped up and ran out the door.

I arrived late and found my way to the only seats still available, in the balcony.

It wasn't long before I realized how different everything was in this place. I immediately sensed the distinctiveness of God. In the music, in the message, and in the mingling afterward, it was clear that God, not I, was the guest of honor there. Having suffered the bankruptcy of our society's emphasis on self-fulfillment, I was remarkably refreshed to discover a place that focused on the centrality of God.

I didn't understand everything the preacher said that morning, and I didn't like all the songs that were sung. But at that point the style

of the service and what people were wearing became nonissues. They could have all looked Amish or all like hipsters from Brooklyn; they could have been singing old songs or new songs—it didn't matter. Why? Because that morning I encountered something I couldn't escape, something more joltingly powerful than anything I'd ever experienced, something that went above and beyond typical externals. Through both the music and the message, the transcendent presence of God punctured the roof, leaving me—like Isaiah when he entered the temple—awestruck and undone.

I was on the receiving end of something infinitely larger than grand impressions of human talent. God was on full display. It was God, not the preacher or the musicians, who was being lifted up for all to see. It wasn't some carefully orchestrated performance (which, believe me, I would have seen right through). Rather, the people of God were simply honoring God as God.

In the Bible the glory of God is God's "heaviness," his powerful presence. It is God's prevailing excellence on display. That's what I encountered that morning. I met a God who is majestically and brilliantly in command.

I was a seeker being reached, not by a man-centered, trendy show, but by a God-centered, transcendent atmosphere. I was experiencing what Ed Clowney, the late president of Westminster Theological Seminary, used to call "doxological evangelism." It was, quite literally, out of this world.

Here, finally, was the radical difference I'd been longing for.

After the service I couldn't leave. I had to stick around and find out who these people were. As I talked with some of them, I was struck by how different they seemed from the group I'd been out with the night before (or any other night, for that matter). The people here seemed more solid, less superficial, more real, more grounded. They asked me questions. They listened. They genuinely cared about one another—and me. They were indisputably peculiar, in a refreshing way.

Back in my apartment that afternoon, I thought long and hard

about what had made my experience that morning so magnificently satisfying. What stood out most was just how refreshingly different it was, compared to everything I'd come to believe was cool and in style. In fact, according to the culturally fashionable standards I'd come to embrace, everything I had encountered in church that morning was delectably unfashionable.

I had not only encountered radically different people, but through those people I had encountered a radically different God—and as a result I could sense that I was being pulled in a radically different direction. The profound difference I had experienced that morning had already made a profound difference in my life—a difference that would last forever.

I couldn't wait to go back the next week.

Looking for What?

It's been many years since that riveting morning in church. Now I'm a pastor trying to reach the kind of person I used to be. So I reflect on that time in my life and ponder, *What was I looking for? And why?*

My experience in church that morning convinced me that serious seekers today aren't looking for something appealing and trendy. They're looking for something deeper than what's currently in fashion.

The point I want to drive home in this book is that *Christians make a difference in this world by being different from this world; they don't make a difference by being the same.*

This is critically important, because in our trend-chasing world it's tempting for Christians to slowly lose their distinctiveness by accommodating to culture. But by trying so hard to fit in, many Christians risk having nothing distinctive to say to those who feel, in Walker Percy's memorable phrase, "lost in the cosmos."

In contrast, I'm asking you to embrace the delicious irony Christ demonstrated in bringing a message of God's kingdom that subversively transforms both individuals and the world. Only by being properly unfashionable can we engage our broken world with an embodied gospel that witnesses to God's gracious promise of restoration, significance, and life.

As you'll come to see in the pages ahead, by *unfashionable* I'm not talking about what you wear or how you look, the lingo you use or the music you listen to. I'm talking about something deeper, more significant—and much more demanding.

I want to help you reimagine the potential impact of a radically unfashionable lifestyle. I want to show you what God-soaked, gospel-infused priorities look like in relationships, community, work, finances, and culture—and how those priorities can change the world. I'm hoping you'll work your way through this book (and the study guide at the back) and gain a clearer picture of what it means to live subversively—and redemptively—for God and his expanding kingdom. My earnest prayer is that this book will help to mobilize a generation of God-saturated missionaries who will live *against the world for the world*.

So let's get started.

A World Without Windows

> Color blindness is the apt metaphor for some: They
> miss the rich-hued splendor of the spiritual vision of
> life and see only the colder, duller world of black and
> white.
>
> —OS GUINNESS

● ● ● ● ● ●

IF YOU'RE LIKE MOST PEOPLE, you think our culture today has the most expanded vistas ever—the most wide-open perspectives, the most enlightened outlooks.

But think again.

People in the twenty-first century are living in a "world without windows," to borrow a phrase from sociologist Peter Berger.[1] In previous eras people lived with "windows" opening out from life in this world. Most cultures generally accepted a larger purpose beyond the immediate, and they recognized the higher power of something supernatural. As Os Guinness notes, "The deepest experiences of all were held to be 'religious,' 'sacred,' 'other,' or 'transcendent,' however these terms were defined."[2]

But in recent times technological advances and scientific expansion have increasingly succeeded in shutting the windows and closing the blinds. The physical replaces the spiritual, the temporal replaces the eternal, and "what is seen" replaces what is unseen (Hebrews 11:3).

In this windowless world, God, transcendence, and mystery have become less and less imaginable. All of life is "rationalized."

Everything becomes a matter of human classification, calculation, and control. "What counts in a rationalized world," says Guinness, "is efficiency, predictability, quantifiability, productivity, the substitution of technology for the human, and—from first to last—control over uncertainty."[3] Everything's produced, managed, and solved this side of the ceiling, which explains why so many people are restless and yearning, as I was, for meaning that transcends this world—for something and Someone *different*.

This may be why every television season seems to bring new supernatural dramas, such as *Ghost Whisperer, Supernatural,* and *Heroes.* And why people are increasingly fascinated with Eastern mysticism, angels, aliens, psychics, the afterlife, and metaphysical healing. Our generation is crying out for something different, something higher, something beyond this world. They long for elements that a world without windows disallows—mystery, transcendence, and a deep sense of wonder, awe, and spirituality. "Eternal questions and yearnings," says Guinness, "are thrusting their way up between the cracks in the sterile world of secular disenchantment."[4]

Hungry for the Timeless

Moreover, because today's world is in a constantly accelerating state of flux—always changing, never staying the same—people crave constancy and depth. Such painful impermanence makes people open to, and desirous for, things truthful and historical, ancient and proven. As one cultural critic observed, "From the historic preservation movement to the nostalgia of popular culture with its TV reruns, historical fiction, and 'retro' fashions, contemporary people are fascinated and attracted to the past."[5]

In a recent study conducted by LifeWay Research, unchurched Americans indicated that they preferred more traditional-looking church buildings by a nearly two-to-one ratio over the generic warehouselike structures built in recent decades. "Quite honestly, this research surprised us," said Ed Stetzer, director of LifeWay Research and missiologist-in-residence for LifeWay Christian Resources. "We expected they'd choose the more contemporary options, but they were clearly more drawn to the aesthetics of the Gothic building than the run-of-the-mill, modern church building."[6] Stetzer believes (rightly, in my view) that unchurched Americans may be drawn to the look of old cathedrals because they speak to a connectedness to the past.

People in today's world are desperately reaching, not just upward, but backward. They yearn for a day gone by when things seemed more constant and less shallow. They want to tap into treasures of the past as they search for a staying power that seems unattainable in the present.

Ironically, our culture's rejection of absolute truth is stoking an unprecedented hunger for truth. In his book *Surprising Insights from the Unchurched,* Thom Ranier reveals interesting discoveries that highlight the contemporary thirst for truth. More than 85 percent of the unchurched people Ranier surveyed said that a church's theology and doctrine would be their primary consideration in choosing a church. Not music, not entertainment, but theology—truth. New generations are thirsting for truthfulness, not trendiness. They long for someone to speak to them truthfully about a time and a place other than their own, about something and someone other than themselves. They want to know that there are different people out there with their sights set on a different world.

Through personal experience people have realized that the modern world's unwavering claim that mass information leads inevitably to mass transformation is an empty lie. I've talked to many people who are becoming increasingly wary of the latest techno trend. They complain of how impersonal and disenchanting modern life has become. They're weary of both the messages and the methods being churned out by the marketing machines in today's world.

That's why if you stop and listen, you'll hear that the cry of our times is for something completely otherworldly. People are up to their necks in up-to-date structures and cutting-edge methodologies.

They're beginning to understand that modern capabilities cannot make us better and more satisfied people nor make this world a better, more satisfying place. They seem desperate to recover a world that once was, a world that allows for mystery, miracle, and wonder—a world with windows to somewhere else.

This shouldn't be surprising to Christ followers. As Romans 1 teaches us, once we ignore God, we inevitably misuse the goods of creation as we mistakenly make our own rules. So our sin in the vertical direction (ignoring God) inevitably causes disorientation on the horizontal level (as we lose our sense of reference and direction).

The Irrelevance of Relevance

As believers in Christ, we should celebrate these yearnings among today's generation, for their longing is for something only Christ can truly offer. We should be ecstatic that our culture is getting "vertical," yearning for something different from what this world offers. This great cultural crisis brings a great Christian opportunity.

But here's my concern: many church leaders have been telling us for a long time that the church's cultural significance *ultimately* depends on its ability to keep up either with changing structures and environments (innovative technology, for instance) or with the latest intellectual fad (such as postmodernism).

Recently I was flipping through a couple of well-known Christian magazines. I counted six full-page advertisements for upcoming conferences designed to help churches adapt in order to meet modern needs—"new ways for new days." Some emphasized improved techniques, programs, methods, and advertising strategies. Others stressed our need to "emerge" from preoccupation with traditional truth claims and theology and to focus instead on what's *most* important—relationships, caring for the poor, and social justice issues—forgetting that robust theological confession (belief) and Christlike practical compassion (behavior) are always meant to go hand in hand. To believe otherwise is like arguing that the wing on the right side of an airplane is more important than the wing on the left. Without both working together, the plane isn't going anywhere.

Here's what struck me: all this comes at precisely the time when our culture is growing weary of slick production and whatever's new and is growing hungry for authentic presence and historical rootedness. Younger generations don't want trendy engagement from the church; in fact, they're suspicious of it. Instead they want truthful engagement with historical and theological solidity that enables meaningful interaction with transcendent reality. They want desperately to invest their lives in something worth dying for, not some here-today-gone-tomorrow fad.

It's both sad and ironic that this shift is now putting the church in the wrong place at the right time. Just when our culture is yearning for something different, many churches are developing creative ways to be the same. Just as many in our culture are beginning to search back in time, many churches are pronouncing the irrelevance of the past. Just as people are starting to seek after truth, many churches are turning away from it. As a result these churches are losing their distinct identity as a people set apart to reach the world.

I have good news for all of us who are becoming weary of this pressure from church leaders to fit in with the world: *we don't have to.* The relevance of the church doesn't depend on its ability to identify the latest cultural trends and imitate them, whatever they might be. "The ultimate factor in the church's engagement with society," Guinness says, "is the church's engagement with God,"[7] not the church's engagement with the latest intellectual or corporate fashion. Contrary to what we've been hearing, our greatest need as twenty-first-century churches is not structural but spiritual. Our main problem is not that we're culturally out of touch; it's that we're theologically out of tune.

We need to remember that God has established his church as an alternative society, not to compete with or copy this world, but to offer a refreshing alternative to it. When we forget this, we inadvertently communicate to our culture that we have nothing unique to offer, nothing deeply spiritual or profoundly transforming. Tragically, this leaves many in our world looking elsewhere for the difference they crave.

Not long ago *World* magazine featured a cover story entitled "NextGen Worship." It highlighted specific ways in which churches and pastors are trying to reach contemporary people by "fitting in." A response—entitled "Why I Walked Out of Church"—came from Julie R. Neidlinger, who is single, thirty-four, and a writer/artist.

> I'm not going to be one of those starched-collar Christians who, based on personal preference, say that this is a sign we're going to hell in a handbasket and that all things are wrong unless they are done as they were with the Puritans. What I'm saying is that I can't stand the phoniness, or trendiness, or sameness—or whatever I'm trying to say here—that the church seems to catch onto at the tail end, not even aware of how lame it is. The fact that this is not only actually successful in appealing to people, but attracts them, also disgusts me.
>
> It makes me want to throw up.
>
> It's buying into some kind of lie or substitution of cool culture as being relevant when it isn't.
>
> If I see another cool Bible college student or pastoral studies major wearing the hemp choker necklace, flip-flops, open-at-the-collar shirt that's untucked, and baggy jeans, saying words like "dude" and "sweet," I will kick their…. It's like the Christian version of annoying hipsters, an overly-studied and homogenized "with-it" faux coolness.[8]

World magazine writer Mickey McLean saw Julie's response to the cover story and wrote:

> I wouldn't be surprised if there are a lot of Julie Neidlingers out there trying to avoid all the trendiness…. Maybe the

evangelical church should listen more to the Julies of this
world instead of demographic and marketing studies. Then,
maybe they'll keep people like her who are looking for spiritual depth from walking out the back door.[9]

To be clear, the overarching concern for Julie is *not* what a pastor
wears or how he speaks. For her, those are just indicators of a deeper,
more disturbing trend. What really bothers her—and multitudes like
her—is how fascinated many Christians are with adapting to whatever
our world deems to be cool. What many like Julie long to see are
courageous church leaders who don't care whether they fit in, who
dare to be countercultural, and who, like John the Baptist, will serve
as a voice crying out in the wilderness.

Ironically, the more we Christians pursue worldly relevance, the
more we'll render ourselves irrelevant to the world around us. There's
an irrelevance to pursuing relevance, just as there's a relevance to prac-
ticing irrelevance. To be truly relevant, you have to say things that are
unfashionably eternal, not trendy. It's the timeless things that are most
relevant to most people, and we dare not forget this fact in our pursuit of relevance.

In an article about younger generations returning to tradition,
Lauren Winner notes that young people today "are not so much wary
of institutions as they are wary of institutions that don't do what they
are supposed to do."[10] What Christians are "supposed to do" is remind
our culture that the things of this world aren't all there is and that
human beings aren't left to the resources of this world to satisfy our
otherworldly longings. Christians alone can provide our culture with
that longed-for transcendent difference, because only the Christian
gospel offers a true spirituality, an otherworldliness grounded in reality and history. Only the Christian story fuses past, present, and future
with meaning from above and beyond. That's what we have to offer
and proclaim.

Remember, from chapter 1, how I woke up after a night of hard partying and went to church, never to be the same again? As I reflect on what changed me that morning (and what can change others), I've concluded it was the out-of-this-world realization that God is God and I am not—that he's big and I'm small. That's a realization no human strategy, structure, or fashion can reveal. We can't engineer God's transcendent presence; we can only fall on our faces and beg for it. In fact, we rob this world of the opportunity to see God high and lifted up—above and beyond us—when we try to program him and fit him into contemporary categories of "cool." When the size of God grips us more than the size of our churches and leadership conferences, and when we become obsessed with surrendering our lives to God's sovereign presence, only then will we be redemptively different and serve as God's cosmic change agents in a world yearning for change.

We Christians have been entrusted with an eternal, transcendent truth that can transform our weary culture and open others' eyes to a world beyond their own: the story of a simple Jew who made a difference *because* he was different.

And that's where *our* difference starts.

Seduced by Cool

He who marries today's fashion is tomorrow's widow.

—CHARLES SPURGEON

●●●●●●

ACCORDING TO JESUS, Christianity is not cool.

There, I said it.

I'll even go a step farther: if what's fashionable in our society interests you, then true Christianity won't. It's that simple.

Think about it. Jesus said some pretty unfashionable stuff. *If you want to live, you must die. If you want to find your life, you must lose it.* He talked about self-sacrifice and bearing crosses and suffering and death and the dangers of riches. He talked about the need to lay down our lives for those who hate us and hurt us. He talked about serving instead of being served, about seeking last place and not first. He talked of gouging out our eyes and cutting off our hands if they cause us to sin.

He was making the profound point that daily Christian living means daily Christian dying—dying to our fascination with the sizzle of this world and living for something bigger, something thicker, something eternal. Jesus calls his people to live for what is timeless and not trendy, to take up the cross and follow him, even when it means going against social norms.

Of course, all this is flat-out uncool in a world that idolizes whatever cultural craze is in style, whatever is fashionable.

This prayer from Arthur Bennett presents the paradoxical nature of God's ways in contrast to the world's:

Let me learn by paradox
that the way down is the way up,
that to be low is to be high,
that the broken heart is the healed heart,
that the contrite spirit is the rejoicing spirit,
that the repenting soul is the victorious soul,
that to have nothing is to possess all,
that to bear the cross is to wear the crown,
that to give is to receive,
that the valley is the place of vision.[1]

In God's upside-down economy, the road to the top is from the bottom—and that flies in the face of everything our culture believes is necessary to be successful. To be successful, we're told, we must seek after power, wealth, recognition, status. But what we find in the Bible is a God who explains success in terms of giving, not taking; self-sacrifice, not self-indulgence; going to the back, not getting to the front; faithfulness, not fashion.

In fact, almost everything Jesus said about the nature of Christian discipleship is precisely the opposite of what our culture exalts.

Blessed?

Take the Beatitudes, where Jesus (in Matthew 5:3–12) describes the characteristics of those who truly follow him. When you compare these traits to what our world commonly values, you clearly see the upside-down nature of God's ways.

Blessed are the poor in spirit? Our culture looks down on those who aren't self-sufficient, self-reliant, and self-made. It commends those who are "rich in spirit."

Blessed are those who mourn? We tend to dismiss those who acknowledge the dark reality of their own sin. They're psychologically unhealthy, and their real problem is a lack of self-esteem.

Blessed are the meek? We exalt the socially strong and influential—

the powerbrokers. After all, what do we see more of—conferences on serving or conferences on leading?

Blessed are the merciful? Blessed are the peacemakers? Mercy and peacemaking appear weak; revenge is tougher, more honorable. After winning a game by forty-two points, a famous basketball player was asked why his team's starting lineup stayed in after the outcome was certain. He replied, "You don't get anywhere in this world by having sympathy."

Blessed are the pure in heart? What could possibly be more old-fashioned (or judgmental) than purity? People who pursue moral cleanness are either labeled as self-righteous or considered to be naively out of touch with modern society.

Jesus goes on to say that if we're serious about following him down this countercultural road, the world will insult us, persecute us, and tell lies about us (vv. 10–11). In other words, we won't be very popular.

That's what this book is all about—being unfashionable.

For Losers, Not Winners

In a recent interview I was asked if I saw any troubling trends among today's young Christians.

I answered, "Our fascination with fitting in."

Having concluded that the best way to reach the world is to become more like it, many professing Christians strive to think, believe, and act like the world. We become preoccupied with persuading the world around us that we're cool, that we can "hang." The implication, of course, is that Jesus would do those things too. So we go out of our way to prove we're just as smart and stylish, just as successful and savvy, just as powerful and prosperous as the world. In a word, we want the world around us to conclude that Christians can be winners too. But in doing this we're forgetting the key truth that "fame in this country [heaven] and fame on Earth are two quite different things," as C. S. Lewis put it in *The Great Divorce*.[2]

The truth is that real Christianity is good news for losers, not winners (see Luke 5:31–32). The true power of the Christian faith is human weakness, not strength.

> For consider your calling, brothers: not many of you were
> wise according to worldly standards, not many were
> powerful, not many were of noble birth. But God chose
> what is foolish in the world to shame the wise; God
> chose what is weak in the world to shame the strong;
> God chose what is low and despised in the world, even
> things that are not, to bring to nothing things that are,
> so that no human being might boast in the presence of
> God. (1 Corinthians 1:26–29)

The cross is the supreme revealer of the radical difference between this world's values and the values of God. "On the cross," writes Tim Keller, "Christ wins through losing, triumphs through defeat, achieves power through weakness and service, comes to wealth via giving all away."[3] All this demonstrates that *Christians make a difference in the world by being different from it, not by being the same.* Our calling to be in the world but not of the world is what gives us transforming influence. We're to be against the world for the world, as Jesus was, realizing that the power of the Christian faith is the power of the cross, a power that's counterintuitively tied to human weakness.

Instead of trying our best to fit in, we need to be encouraged and challenged by the biblical reminder that God's people have always served the world around them best when they've been countercultural, shaped by God's unfashionable ways to such a degree that they're distinctively different from the world.

A Loss of Trust

Sadly, it's just this point of being different that many in the church seem to be resisting more and more.

Back in the 1950s, when my grandfather was becoming a well-known preacher of the gospel, a famous actor pulled him aside and said, "Billy, don't ever try to compete with Hollywood, because Hollywood will always do it better than you. You give the world the one thing Hollywood can't—the straightforward, timeless truth of the gospel." For more than sixty years, that's exactly what he did.

In many ways the church today needs to heed that actor's advice. Many Christians have lost faith in God's unfashionable ways. We've spent too much time and money trying to "be Hollywood" so we'll fit in.

Not to be outdone by the world around us, we've entered into competition with it. In some circles, the transformation of gospel proclamation into entertainment is quickly becoming the standard, not the exception. Pastors outdo each other in becoming as fashionable and smooth as any performer on Broadway. Furthermore, we've developed a "Christian" imitation of everything in pop culture. Walk into many Christian bookstores and you'll find "Christian" T-shirts (instead of Abercrombie & Fitch, it's Abreadcrumb & Fish), "Christian" candy (Testamints, for example), and "Christian" board games and toys (such as the Jesus action figure my son received from a friend for his birthday; I immediately took it away for fear that Jesus would eventually be engaged in a fight with Darth Vader and lose).

Even contemporary Christian music groups intentionally imitate non-Christian bands. One Christian bookstore I visited offered a comparison list of Christian bands and their secular counterparts: "If you like the Dave Matthews Band, you'll love…" or "If you love Beyoncé, you'll love…" Of course the store owner is just trying to use common cultural reference points to move product that might deliver a more redeeming musical experience. But this kind of mimicry hides a larger problem.

In his book *All God's Children and Blue Suede Shoes,* Ken Myers argues that Christians by and large have responded to the surrounding culture by developing a look-alike culture. Instead of creating something new, something refreshingly different, we Christians seem content to copy the world around us. Even in the realm of ideas, many expressions of Christianity have become indistinguishable from some of our world's intellectual trends regarding truth, knowledge, and morality (more on this later).

In the words of author Paul Grant, many Christians have been "seduced by cool."

Of course this is nothing new. The ancient Israelites rejected God as their king in favor of a human king "such as all the other nations have" (1 Samuel 8:5, NIV). God's people have always struggled with wanting to fit in.

This is a weakness we must overcome. The faithful, according to Jesus, are not intended to be fashionable. They're not supposed to fit in. They're called out from the world to be "odd." Our oddness, in fact, is essential to our faithfulness. To put it another way, faithfulness to Christ requires foreignness to the world's trendy diversions.

In C. S. Lewis's fictional *The Screwtape Letters,* the senior demon Screwtape advises a demon in training to keep Christians "in the state of mind I call 'Christianity And.'" For his 1940s audience, Lewis illustrated this by "Christianity and the New Psychology, Christianity and the New Order, Christianity and Faith Healing," and others. Today such a list would be topped by "Christianity and Coolness."

Screwtape goes on to say that if people must be Christians, let them be Christians with a diversion. "Substitute for the faith itself some Fashion with a Christian colouring. Work on their horror of the Same Old Thing."[4] Mere Christianity ("the Same Old Thing") just doesn't seem fashionable enough all by itself, so we try spicing it up with some up-to-the-minute cachet.

Today more than ever Christians need to be reminded of the antithesis between the wisdom of the world and the wisdom of God (see 1 Corinthians 1–3). Much of what the world esteems as wise, God considers foolish; much of what the world dismisses as foolish, God considers wise.

As we'll see, true followers of Jesus have been given a new heart and mind, a new way, a new destiny. This is why we're to operate according to a different standard, with different goals and motivations and an altogether different perspective on money, lifestyle, and relationships. Our thoughts, our affections, our behavior, our priorities and pursuits and passions—all are to be different. We're to march to the beat of a different drummer.

The World: Love It or Hate It? *We are the world*

Since I've cast "the world" in a rather negative light, let me explain what I mean and don't mean by that phrase.

Have you ever wondered why the Bible seems to be guilty of double-talk when speaking of the world? John 3:16 tells us that God the Father loves the world so much that he sent God the Son to fix it. But we're told in 1 John 2:15–17 *not* to love the world, and James tells us that "a friend of the world" is "an enemy of God" (James 4:4). We have Paul telling us in 2 Corinthians 6:17 to be separate from the world and to "go out from" unbelievers, while Jesus in Mark 16:15 commands his disciples to "go into all the world." *(worldliness)*

What's going on? Is the world good or bad? Are we to love it or hate it? Enter it or exit it?

The answer: it all depends on which sense of the word *world* you mean.

As scholars point out, the word *world* has three basic meanings in the Bible. It can refer to (1) the created order, (2) the human community, and (3) the sinful ways of humanity, or cultural godlessness. It's this third meaning, for instance, that Paul identifies when he tells us, "Do not be conformed to [the *patterns of*] *this world,* but be transformed by the renewal of your mind" (Romans 12:2). He's not telling us to avoid the created order or other human beings. It's actually *worldliness* that Paul is warning against.

Furthermore, when it comes to *the world,* it's necessary to differentiate between structure and direction. It's the difference between *what* there is and *how* we use what there is. The world as structure refers to the people (such as my next-door neighbor), places (such as Miami), and things (such as art or music) of the created order. *Direction* refers to the ethical use or misuse of God's created goods. As we'll explore later, God created all things good (structure). But our sin has broken and corrupted every good thing God created, "directing" it away from him. Everything in the created order (every person, place, and thing) has been twisted out of shape by our sin.

Sex, for instance, is a structural good that God has built into his creation, while sex outside marriage is an ethical misuse of that good. Or, to take an example one of my friends uses, the storytelling ability of movies is a structural good that's a part of God's created order (God himself is a storyteller). But the illicit sex, perverse humor, and shallow story lines found in many movies represent an ethical misuse of that created good. Therefore, while God loves the structure of the world (Creation), he hates its sinful direction (the Fall), though he's now in the process of redirecting it back toward himself (redemption).

We are, of course, to follow God's lead in this. We're to love the world's structure (peoples, places, and things) while fighting against the world's sinful direction. Or, as Flannery O'Connor put it, if you are a Christian, "you have to cherish the world at the same time that you struggle to endure it."[5]

Worldliness, then, is characterized in the Bible as the sinful misdirection of God's good creation. It means adopting the ways, habits, thought patterns, practices, spirit, and tastes of this world in spite of how far they take us from God's will and design. We become conformed to the patterns of this world when the ways we think and live fit in nicely with how this fallen, misdirected world thinks and lives. Worldliness is what makes the world's ways seem normal and God's ways seem strange. *very pro found!*

Christians have often reduced worldliness to a catalog of bad behaviors—drinking, smoking, dancing, going to movies, getting a tattoo, or whatever the current list of taboos includes in your community. But that's not the primary biblical definition. In the Bible worldliness is exposed as an internal, invisible problem before it's an external, visible problem, which makes it much harder to detect. The challenge of worldliness is that its influence goes largely unnoticed. It seeps in like the tide rather than crashing in like a tidal wave.

A worldly way of thinking is any mind-set that, unconsciously or consciously, eliminates God and his revealed truth (the Bible) from how we approach life. The biblical notion of worldliness is a sleepiness of the soul in which the status, pleasures, comforts, and cares of the world appear solid, stunning, and affecting while the truths of Scripture become abstractions—unable to grip the heart or guide our everyday activities. Worldliness, according to Iain Murray, "is departing from God. It is a man-centered way of thinking.... It judges the importance of things by the present and material results. It weighs success by numbers. It covets human esteem, and it wants no unpopularity. It knows no truth for which it is worth suffering. It declines to be a fool for Christ's sake."[6]

To be a worldly person is, in fact, to be a "practical" or "functional" atheist. It's someone who—despite all he professes—lives and makes daily decisions as if God doesn't exist. A practical atheist is a person who comes to conclusions about money, business, worship, entertainment, ministry, education, or whatever else without the directing influence of God and his revealed truth (the Bible). Instead, for him, cultural assumptions and societal trends serve as the directing influences for how he thinks, feels, and lives.

Worldliness, as I've explained it, seems to have two components: vertical and horizontal. The vertical component is living for self rather than God. The horizontal component is sinfully corrupting society and culture (misdirecting the structural goods of creation).

Against Worldliness for the World

If we Christians live unaware of the subtle ways in which worldliness seeps into how we think, feel, and live, we'll never exhibit the beautiful, refreshing, unfashionable difference this world desperately needs to see.

When Christians choose not to be different, the seasoning, warming, coloring beauty of Christ gets lost—and the oh-so-fashionable world turns gray and drab, cold and ugly.

I'm not saying, of course, that rejecting worldliness means one must remain culturally clueless. Just the opposite in fact. To avoid being pressed into the world's mold, every Christ follower must work at gaining an accurate understanding of how culture works—where and how it influences the way we think and live. Part of the power of worldliness is that it disguises its influence by becoming the invisible matrix of our lives. We therefore need to recognize the unconscious patterns of worldliness so we can resist their toxic influence. This can happen only if we develop a cultural radar—something I hope this book will assist you in.

Failing this, we have no hope of being the salt and light Christ called us to be in and for the world. In fact, as theologian David Wells reminds us, it is "those who are cognitively and morally dislocated from worldly culture" who alone carry the power to change it.[7]

Our being cognitively and morally entrenched in the ways of this world is just what the devil wants. His main strategy is the same for both Christians and non-Christians: keep them feeling comfortably at home in this world. The real danger for many of us is that the longer we live, the less conscious we become of this world's fallen patterns. And the less conscious we become of the fallen patterns, the less resistant we are to their entanglements. Though believers in Christ, many of us are attached to the world in ways that show we've forgotten our identity as exiles. For too many of us, the patterns of this fallen world have grown all too familiar, while the ways of God seem distant and strange.

But Christians are to be governed by what the Lord says, not by what the world says. We're to pattern our ideas, beliefs, methods, and tastes in accordance with God's ways rather than the world's. Our calling in this world is to be God's otherworldly representatives, to serve as his "city on a hill," his light in these shadows, his hope in this world of brokenness. We're to be a counterculture for the common good—to live against the world for the world.

I want to be part of a generation that understands this and is radically committed to being different, unfashionable, uncool. This is our privileged calling—yours and mine—and our present opportunity.

Our mission begins with our embrace of an unfashionable standard.

Part 2

The C●mmission

An Unfashionable Standard

> The Holy Scriptures are the lifeline God throws us in
> order to ensure that he and we stay connected while
> the rescue is in progress.
>
> —J. I. PACKER

NOT LONG AGO I WAS IN NEW YORK having dinner with a friend who's
not a Christian. We enjoy getting together, in part because there's
always a great mixture of seriousness and silliness in our conversations.
We love to talk about politics, family, and sports (he's a die-hard New
York Giants fan; I'm all for the Dallas Cowboys).

At some point, at his initiative, every conversation seems to turn
toward what I believe and why. On this particular occasion he said,
"You Christians always talk about using the Bible as your standard for
everything—your guide for the way you live. I mean, seriously, what's
your fascination with that outdated book?"

I told him Christians aren't the only people who use standards to
govern their lives. Everyone does it; everyone appeals to some authority when determining how to navigate their lives.

"Not me," he said.

Curious, I asked how he decided what to live for and how he
determined right from wrong, good from bad, truth from lies.

"I go with my gut," he answered. "My instincts. I certainly don't
need an antiquated book to help me do it."

"So it's not that I govern my life according to a standard while you do not," I said. "Apparently the real difference between us is that you're serving as your own standard, and I appeal to the Bible as mine." Somewhat grudgingly, he conceded the point.

The truth is, we're all influenced by something or someone as we navigate our lives. We all let factors that are external (outside advice) or internal (past experience or prejudices) play a role when we decide what job to take, how to parent our kids, or what to do with our money. We all draw on something when deciding how to live and what choices to make. The question is, to what are you looking for guidance? What ultimate authority is informing you and influencing your choices and conclusions?

We may think there's quite a range of possible answers for such a question, but they actually boil down to two: we're being guided either by the wisdom of this world or by the wisdom of God. It's that simple.

My conversation with my friend reveals the fact that we live in a culture seeking to convince us that man is the measure of all things—each of us alone is captain of our fate and master of our soul. We're told it's far more fashionable to be our own guide, to develop our own standards, to operate according to our own rules, and to come to our own conclusions. This is pounded into our lives relentlessly (and seductively) through Madison Avenue marketing. It's the mantra of the titans of business and the siren song of Hollywood's "beautiful people." The most current "wisdom" seems much more up-to-date, relevant, and reliable than the seemingly outdated wisdom revealed by God.

Yet Christians have always been called by God to be people of the Book, regardless of how outmoded that rule might seem to others. The Bible is God's manual on how to live unfashionably. We're to be constantly asking, "What does the Bible say?" and then living and choosing accordingly.

Sola Scriptura

During the Protestant Reformation in the sixteenth century, five Latin phrases emerged as summary statements to identify core Christian beliefs: *sola Scriptura* (Scripture alone), *sola fide* (faith alone), *sola gratia* (grace alone), *solus Christus* (Christ alone), and *soli Deo gloria* (glory to God alone).

The first of these phrases, sola Scriptura, laid the foundation for the others. For in the Bible we encounter the truth that we're saved by grace alone, through faith alone, in the finished work of Christ alone, so that God alone gets all the glory for our rescue. But the main point of sola Scriptura is that the Bible (both Old and New Testaments) serves as the fullest and highest God-given and authoritative standard by which we're to govern our thinking and living. The Bible is to be our guide. We're to think the way the Bible teaches us to think and to live the way the Bible teaches us to live. We're to cherish what the Bible values and reject what the Bible warns against. Our tastes, methods, and perspectives on everything are meant to be informed and shaped by what the Bible says.

Further, sola Scriptura means that the Word of God is sufficient. For many of us this is where sola Scriptura stings a bit.

Reliable, Yes…but Relevant?

Not long ago I was asked by the women in our church to speak to them about the role of the Bible in the life of the Christian. I began by saying that when it comes to the Bible, most Christians have no struggle with its reliability. We believe it's the Word of God—not, as some might claim, a man-made book, but a God-made book.

We're sure that "all Scripture is breathed out by God" (2 Timothy 3:16), that God is the Bible's ultimate author, though he employed human writers such as Moses, David, Isaiah, and Paul. We confess that these God-selected humans wrote precisely what God wanted them to write so that we have exactly what he intended us to have.

Furthermore, Christians have historically affirmed both the Bible's infallibility (it's an absolutely sure and safe guide from God in all matters of life) and its inerrancy (it's entirely true and entirely free from any mistakes). We have no problem affirming its perfect truthfulness.

But most of us do struggle when it comes to the Bible's timelessness, its relevance.

That's because God and his Word have been relegated to the fringe of what's important and defining in our society, a process identified by the term *secularization*. A secularized society is one that has determined to make what God says socially irrelevant, even if it remains personally engaging. It restricts the relevance of God to the private sphere. This has created, according to Richard John Neuhaus, "a naked public square"; God's Word may be alive and well privately, but publicly, socially, and culturally, it's dead.

In *The Abolition of Man,* C. S. Lewis noted one consequence of this cultural death of God's Word: if we remove God and his Word from the public square, we leave people without the capacity to make moral judgments about the world. Stripped of the divine resource we need to discern between the ultimately true and the ultimately false, everything becomes a matter of private opinion. This creates what Lewis calls "men without chests." It produces a less-than-robust person (which in turn produces a less-than-robust society) who is too weak to make absolute moral judgments and uncompromising moral stands.

This cultural death of God and his Word can be seen in just about every sector of society: science, technology, politics, economics, art, corporate relationships, and even the church.

In effect, many of us followers of Christ have become just as secular as the world around us. We've been suckered into thinking that what God has to say isn't nearly as relevant as what the world around us is saying. So even though we may embrace the Bible's integrity, we have a hard time embracing its sufficiency. *After all,* we think, *the Bible's authors didn't face the unique pressures of our modern world, nor did they have access to the technological tools and scientific answers we now have* (revealing our bloated sense of contemporary human insight). Yes, the Bible contains some good and wise principles, but does it have anything to say about real-life challenges and opportunities we face in the modern world?

Many professing Christians, I'm afraid, have concluded that it doesn't. For example, I recently read this statement by Luke Timothy Johnson, New Testament professor at Emory University:

> I think it important to state clearly that we do, in fact, reject the straightforward commands of Scripture, and appeal instead to another authority when we declare that same-sex unions can be holy and good. We appeal explicitly to the weight of our own experience.[1]

This example may seem a bit extreme. But Professor Johnson is simply stating what many professing Christians practice.

I've been a pastor long enough to know that when it comes to the way we think about marriage, parenting, sexual orientation, finances, politics, education, career aspirations, ministry, and even worship, plenty of Christians take their cues, not from what the Bible says, but from gurus like Tony Robbins and Peter Drucker and Oprah and Rush Limbaugh. Therapeutic techniques, marketing strategies, and the beat of the entertainment world often have far more influence over how we live and think, what we like and don't like, than does the Word of God. Just like the world around us, we read self-help books, study the latest pop-culture craze, watch reality TV, and pay attention to the popular opinions of the day on everything from how to have the most satisfying sex life to what we should spend our money on. We absorb the values and worldview of our current culture without ever asking, "What does the Bible say about this?"

We may believe in sola Scriptura in theory, but too often in practice we embrace *sola cultura,* leaving the Bible far behind.

The Enemy Is Us

A friend of mine who's an attorney recently told me about a well-known Christian leader who sued another well-known Christian leader over a property-rights disagreement. My friend had been asked to serve as a mediator. As he explained it, the issue didn't seem irresolvable; the real culprit seemed to be misunderstanding and poor communication. He tried to get these two men together to work out their differences, but they refused to meet, and the lawsuit went forward.

I asked my friend how these two leaders responded to the scriptural teaching that Christians aren't to sue one another. My friend answered grievingly, "What the Bible says never entered into the discussion." He added that this was all too common in his many dealings with Christians. According to him, "the Bible is disregarded completely."

One recent survey found that only a small minority of those who claim to be Christians say they believe in absolute truth. Another survey of professing Christians between the ages of eighteen and thirty-five found that one-third of them had no problem with unmarried men and women sleeping together.

This epidemic of professing Christians ignoring the Bible has led theologian Michael Horton to ask if churches are guilty of secularizing America. Christians are quick, he notes, "to launch public protests against 'secular humanists' for diminishing the role of God in American society," yet "the more likely source of secularization is the church itself."[2] Our first concern should not be (as it too often is) that God is treated so flippantly in American culture but that he is not taken seriously in our own churches. As Pogo famously said, "We have met the enemy, and he is us."

The real tragedy here is that when professing Christians discard the Bible, they're largely prevented from making a lasting difference in the world. Why? Because their standard is no different from the world's. Making that difference requires us to think and live differently than the world does, and the Bible alone—as revealed truth coming from outside us—is where we learn how to do it.

The Bible as Total Truth

I've found that fathering two athletic and competitive boys can be challenging. My boys' passion to win seems at times to overpower every other sensibility. So when I play basketball or football with Gabe and Nate, I'm always aware of my responsibility to coach them with regard to their conduct on the field or court: "Play hard but stay humble." "Encourage your teammates." "Don't get cocky; don't showboat; don't taunt your opponent." And so on. I really want them to understand that being Christian affects the way they approach everything, even sports.

Whether it's athletic competition, entertainment, sex, money, politics, business, art, or science, our faith ought to inform every arena of thought and life. Nowhere does the Bible say the Christian faith is private, partial, and compartmentalized. On the contrary, the Christian faith is public, pervasive, and complete (see 1 Corinthians 10:31). And this faith is to be governed and fueled by God's Word, not merely on Sundays, but every day and in every way.

The Bible teaches that Christians are called by God to "take every thought captive to obey Christ" (2 Corinthians 10:5), to think biblically about *everything*. It means developing a Christian mind to analyze what's going on around us, to understand how the world thinks, and then to offer a distinctively Christian alternative. It means being able to look at the daily newspaper, listen to modern music, or watch the latest films and compare what we encounter to what the Bible teaches. We develop mental habits whereby we "challenge the assumptions of modern culture and apply biblical tests and create biblical proposals," as Chuck Colson has said.[3]

The late Francis Schaeffer wrote, "Christianity is not just a series of truths but *Truth*—Truth about all of reality."[4] The Bible isn't simply a manual for understanding spiritual concepts. It's earthier than that. It provides us with a comprehensive framework for understanding all of reality. It presents an entire worldview, a complete perspective on all of life. It supplies us with an overarching explanation of where we came from (Creation), what's wrong with us and the world we live in (the Fall), and what's the solution to the problem, or how the world can be set right again (redemption). The Bible is, said John Calvin, the "spectacles" by which Christians are to see, interpret, and understand everything from poetry to politics, from sports to science, from wars to worship, from law to leisure.

With the Bible serving us in this way, Christians are equipped to engage in every arena of our culture, every sector of our society, in a distinctively Christian way. Being a Christian involves thoughtful, Bible-based cultural analysis and cultural engagement on all levels. How does God want us to think about things like justice, legislation, the environment, and education? How does he intend for us to engage all these areas in a God-centered, transformative way? What sort of cultural goods does he intend his people to create? We must have a "theology" about everything under the sun. That's what God requires from us. (We'll explore practical aspects of this in part 3.)

Training Manual

In addition to being the book of capital-T Truth, the Bible is also a book of timeless principles and precepts—lessons and instruction on life that teach us what to pursue and what to avoid. The Bible is God's training manual, teaching us how to think and how to develop skills, knowledge, and insight. It tells us what's important and what isn't, what God loves and what he hates.

By its nature the Bible has reformative powers, for by reading it and putting it into practice we become the people God wants us to become. We can't improve God's Word, but his Word most definitely improves us. Because it's sure, it makes us stable. Because it's right, it makes us wise. It informs our minds, enlarges our hearts, and bends our wills. It has the power to fight sin in our lives, the sin that makes us naturally biased, blind, and brash. For all these natural tendencies, the Bible is the corrective. It has the power both to reveal sin and to restrain sin. It exposes our needs for God-centered adjustment in our thinking, our feeling, and our doing. That's how the Bible transforms us.

It has this transformational power because in its pages we encounter not simply ideas but God. Though he unveils himself generally in nature and in everything good and true, in Scripture he reveals himself *specifically*—what he's accomplished in the past, what he's doing in the present, and what he plans to do in the future. The Bible is God's story. In its pages we learn about God's unfolding plan to restore a broken world. In the words of J. I. Packer, the Bible reveals God "as more than a distant cosmic architect...or an impersonal life-force.... He is the living God, present and active everywhere."[5] Packer reminds us to "think of the Bible as a listening post where you go to hear the voice of God."[6]

Besides revealing the truth about God, the Bible reveals the truth about us—who we are and how we're to live. It's where God clarifies what our priorities, passions, and pursuits ought to be. It's where he encourages us, corrects us, challenges us, comforts us, exhorts us. It's where he offers his children fatherly protection, warning about enemy territory and showing us how to avoid the devil's land mines. And it's where he gives us the power we need to press on—unfashionably.

In the Bible, God personally speaks to us for our good in every way. As Paul tells us in 2 Timothy 3:16–17, all of Scripture is "profitable for teaching, for reproof, for correction, and for training in righteousness, that the man of God may be competent, equipped for *every* good work"—not just spiritual or evangelistic work.

In his book *Truth and Power,* Packer develops the picture of God's Word in Psalm 119:105 as the lamp for our feet and the light for our path:

> You have to take a journey across open country, and it is dark. Traveling in the dark across open country—rough country, too—you are at risk. The easiest thing in the world will be to lose the path, stumble and fall over some obstacle that in the dark you could not see, and do yourself serious mischief. The likelihood of your reaching your destination in the dark is small. However much you squint your eyes and glare into the blackness, you are still unable to see the way to go. There is a path—you know that—but without a light you cannot hope to keep to it. You need a light (it was

oil lamps in the ancient world, but think of a flashlight as what you need today)—and God in his mercy puts one into your hand. You shine it in front of you, and you can see the next bit of the track, so that step by step you know where to put your foot. You walk without stumbling; you follow the path; you move ahead toward your goal.[7]

Trying to follow God's lead without God's light guarantees a life of stumbling.

When the relevance of God's Word reigns supreme among God's set-apart people, we influence the wider culture by expressing his revealed truth with both our lives and our lips. Let's look closer at what all that means.

The Purpose-Driven Death

> Our sense of purpose as individuals and as a church
> depends largely on how clearly we grasp certain
> truths about who God is, who we are, and what
> God's plan for history involves.
>
> — MICHAEL HORTON

● ● ● ● ● ●

CHOOSING TO LIVE AGAINST THE WORLD for the world can be downright deadly.

Jesus's whole life and ministry testify to this. The Bible tells us that, though he was rich, he became poor. Though he was a king, he became a servant to all. Though he was the strongest, he became weak. And in the end his unwavering devotion to live against the world for the world cost him his life.

But Jesus was able to endure the cross and all its shame because he knew just how powerful and effective his unfashionable life had been (see Hebrews 12:2). He knew his life, death, and resurrection would turn the world upside down, guaranteeing that one day this broken world will be forever fixed.

A certain type of death will be required from us as well if we choose to follow Jesus by living according to God's standards. It will mean taking up the cross daily and dying to our incessant attraction to the ways of this world. When faced with the world's intense pressure, we'll give in and go along unless we, too, are convinced of just how powerful and effectual an unfashionable life can be. Even if we start out strong—on fire for God after a profound conversion experience—we'll quickly lose steam if we don't have a compelling vision fueling us to press on and strain forward against all opposition.

Where would such a compelling vision come from? I believe it can be nothing less than the same vision that compelled Jesus. We need to be aware, as he was, of what God is working to achieve, the direction God is taking. We need to see God's blueprint: what once was, what now is, and what one day will be. God reveals this blueprint in the Bible.

The effectiveness of our unfashionable living is rooted in our deep identification with the *whole* story set forth in the Bible. Our task is to recognize how it all fits together.

The Road to Cosmic Renewal

Essentially the Bible tells a three-part story:

Creation: God made everything good.

Fall: Our sin has broken everything.

Redemption: Everything in Christ will be made new.

In Genesis 1–2 the Bible opens with *creation.* By his powerful, life-giving word, God created the universe out of nothing (*ex nihilo*).

There's a Creator and there's a creation, and they are fundamentally distinct. God is the designer; creation is the designed. God is the definer; creation is the defined. God is independent, while everything God made is dependent upon him. Apart from the Creator, creation cannot exist; apart from the creation, however, the Creator *does* exist. That's the ultimate difference between creation and its Creator. Creation needs the Creator; the Creator does not need the creation.

Furthermore, in Genesis 1:31 we are told that "God saw everything that he had made, and behold, it was very good." God was thoroughly pleased with his creative activity. There was nothing in all creation that did not delight him. His perfect, unblemished fingerprints were on everything—black holes, nebulae, pink salamanders, ice crystals, a leaf bud unfurling in spring, mold, an atomic particle. All of creation was designed to shout, "God!" This is why, as Jeff Purswell rightly points out, "any notion that denigrates the physical world or that carves up reality into sacred versus secular, spiritual versus non-spiritual" is unbiblical, for "the Bible affirms the entire creation as a good gift from God, existing for his glory."[1]

But there's more to this part of the story.

Not only did God create all things good, but unlike anything else in the material world, human beings were specially created and designed by God to live in fellowship with him. Genesis 1:26–27 says, "Then God said, 'Let us make man in our image, after our likeness.…' So God created man in his own image, in the image of God he created him; male and female he created them." Adam and Eve were made in the image of God (*imago Dei*). This means that, like them, we were uniquely created to reflect God in ways that nothing else does. We were, in fact, created to be like God in every way possible for finite creatures to be like him. Our capacities to think, feel, and act were patterned after our Creator—something that cannot be said of trees, oceans, mountains, insects, birds, or any type of animal.

But the *primary* implication of being made in the image of God is that human beings would reflect the creative character of their Maker. This becomes obvious in Genesis 1:28. As his choice creation, God entrusted human beings with the high responsibility of caring for and developing all he had made: "God blessed them and said to them, 'Be fruitful and increase in number; fill the earth and subdue it'" (Genesis 1:28, NIV). Nancy Pearcey calls this directive "the first job description," which implies more than just population growth: "The first phrase, 'be fruitful and multiply,' means to develop the social world: build families, churches, schools, cities, governments, laws. The second phrase, 'subdue the earth,' means to harness the natural world: plant crops, build bridges, design computers, compose music."[2] This job description reveals our global responsibility to "gen-erate a life-affirming, life-sustaining culture in its widest variety—from making babies to making music, from family life to civic life."[3] We were, in other words, put in charge of cultivating and pruning creation, thereby enabling its full potential to glorify its Creator.

Christians often refer to these responsibilities as humanity's "cultural mandate." It was never God's intention for people to have a hands-off approach to the world. From the beginning of time, God purposed that we would make something out of the world; he meant his image bearers to create, to build an earthly culture *for his glory.*

But something happened—something disastrous.

The Test

In Genesis 3 we read about the Fall. Adam and Eve, perfectly representing all of humanity, broke God's good world when they stubbornly chose to be their own god by eating the fruit of the one tree God had told them not to eat from. For Adam and Eve this prohibition was a test from God: "Will you trust me or trust yourself?" Given that the tree was called the tree of the knowledge of good and evil, God was testing them specifically to see if they would rely on his standards for good and evil, truth and beauty, or develop their own. He was testing them to see if they would embrace and forever submit to the fact that all of creation depends on its Creator, not only for physical things, but also for knowledge and moral understanding.

They failed the test.

Contrary to what we read in Philippians 2:6–8 about Jesus (the last Adam), the first Adam grasped for equality with God.

Sadly, it wasn't long before everyone was doing what was right in their own eyes. By the time we reach Genesis 6, we encounter a God who is so distraught by mankind's wicked autonomy that he determines to send a great flood to wipe out all he'd made, except for pairs of every animal and one family from mankind.

Time would repeatedly prove that Adam and Eve's disobedience wasn't an isolated act of disobedience but rather an act of cosmic treason that catastrophically diseased all of God's good creation. Thereafter, according to Romans 8:20, all the created order "was subjected to futility."

Vern Poythress points out the broad wreckage of that futility:

> As a result of the Fall human beings who have descended from Adam suffer sin and death, and end up hurting one another in their sin and misery. But the curse that God pronounces because of Adam's Fall also results in alterations in the broader created order. One thinks of mosquitoes, tapeworms, rabies, all the carriers of diseases so debilitating to human beings. Who can guess all the ways in which the created order may have been put out of joint as a result of the Fall?[4]

Humanity's revolt has perverted everything God created—not only individual human beings, but all of nature and the human community as well. "Like a stone tossed in a pond," says Michael Wittmer, "the corrosive curse of sin rippled out to destroy the entire world: human society, the animal kingdom, and even the ground itself began groaning beneath the weight of sin."[5]

Although this catastrophic fall distorted God's image in mankind, it did not destroy it. Even in our fallen, broken state, we still reflect God in ways that nothing else in creation does. And though our reflection of him may now seem as strangely contorted as that of the image in a carnival mirror, it is a reflection nonetheless.

The same continuation is true when it comes to our cultural mandate. The human responsibility to be fruitful, increase, fill, and subdue—to create culture—was not annulled by the Fall. Sin does not abrogate it. We are still called to be creational caretakers and cultural developers, stewarding all things in a manner that is creative, life affirming, and God exalting. In fact, immediately after the Flood, God repeated the mandate to Noah's family (see Genesis 9:1–7), and it found amplified expression when God, through Abraham, chose a people to be his own, reminding them that they were to "be a blessing" in this world, that in them "all the families of the earth shall be blessed" (Genesis 12:2–3).

So while God's original plan for people to build an earthly culture for his glory may now be corrupted by our attempts to build an earthly culture for *our* glory (like another tower of Babel), the mandate itself remains intact. Human beings have, in fact, been creating culture since the dawn of human history. Because culture making is something we were wired to do, it's inevitable. Every human society is a culture-building venture.

Ever since the Fall, however, much of earthly culture has moved in a sinful direction. We have multiplied and filled the earth, but it's full of our "bad" as well as God's "good." Amazingly, though, instead of God discarding his disobedient and diseased creation (which he would have been perfectly justified in doing), he set a plan in motion to bring it back.

This is where the third part of the story comes in: *redemption*.

Cosmic Good News

In his masterful children's story *The Lion, the Witch, and the Wardrobe*, C. S. Lewis tells of a country, Narnia, which is under the curse of the White Witch. This evil queen places a spell on the land so that it is "always winter and never Christmas." Under her control the future of Narnia looks bleak until word gets out that "Aslan is on the move." In the story Aslan is a noble lion that represents Christ. He is coming to set things straight. He is coming to destroy the White Witch and thus reverse the curse on Narnia. The first signs of Aslan's movement toward this cursed land are that the snow begins to melt and spring is in the air. The cold begins to fade as the sunrays peer through the dark clouds, promising the dawn of a new day. Everything in Narnia begins to change.

To me, this has always been a great picture of what God is up to.

Redemption is God's arrangement to reverse the curse of sin and to renew all things—to restore creation, not destroy it. God is on a mission to reclaim and replenish his corrupted territory, redirecting it back to himself and thereby "making *all things* new" (Revelation 21:5). God created both the physical and the spiritual, and he's going to redeem both the physical and the spiritual. Revelation 11:15 looks ahead to the day when heavenly voices declare, "The kingdom of the world has become the kingdom of our Lord and of his Christ, and he shall reign forever and ever," meaning that God will transform this present world into the world to come. And, according to the Bible, he's doing this "in Christ."

Redemption is what Christians mean when they speak about the gospel. Simply put, the gospel is the good news that everything *in Christ* will be made new. God the Son was born as a baby to accomplish a mission: to recover and repair a world lost and broken by sin. Jesus came to restore the earth to its original purpose: to serve as a theater for the display of God's glory. He's the divine curse-remover and creation-renewer. Christ's substitutionary death on the cross broke the curse of sin and death brought on by Adam's cosmic rebellion. His bodily resurrection from the dead three days later dealt death its final blow, guaranteeing the eventual renewal of all things.

The dimensions of Christ's finished work are both individual *and* cosmic. They range from personal pardon for sin and individual forgiveness to the final resurrection of our bodies and the restoration of the whole world. Now that's good news—gospel—isn't it? If we place our trust in the finished work of Christ, sin's curse will lose its grip on us individually, and we will one day be given a renewed creation. The gospel isn't only about reestablishing a two-way relationship between God and us; it also restores a three-way relationship among God, his people, and the created order. Through Christ's work our relationship with God is restored while creation itself is renewed. This is what theologians mean when they talk about redemption. They're describing this profound, far-reaching work by God.

Of course none of this is available for those who remain disconnected from Jesus. Sin's acidic curse remains on everything that continues to be separated from Christ. We must be united to Christ by placing our trust in his finished work in order to receive and experience all the newness God has promised. For, as John Calvin said, "as long as Christ remains outside of us, and we are separated from him, all that he has suffered and done for the salvation of the human race remains useless and of no value for us."[6] But for all that is united to Christ, everything false, bad, and corrupting will one day be consumed by what is true, good, and beautifying—and this includes the material world.

Renewed, Not Destroyed

Redemption leads to the culmination and climax of the Bible's story as well as to the ultimate vision for the difference we make in this world by living unfashionably.

For a long time now, I've been convinced that the way most Christians think about redemption is influenced more by ancient Greek philosophy than by the Bible. We think of ultimate redemption as being redemption *from* the body, not *of* the body; redemption *from* the world, not *of* the world; redemption *from* the material, not *of* the material. This, however, goes against what the Bible clearly teaches about redemption.

In the Lord's Prayer we see that God's ultimate goal is for earth to become like heaven.

> Our Father in heaven,
>   hallowed be your name.
>   Your kingdom come,
>   your will be done,
>   on earth as it is in heaven. (Matthew 6:9–10)

God's mission is to bring heaven to earth—this planet!

There are many people who believe that God will destroy this present world—all of it—and start over, creating a new world from scratch. As I've talked to people who believe this, most base their conclusion on 2 Peter 3, where the apostle Peter says, "The heavens and earth that now exist are stored up for fire, being kept until the day of judgment and destruction of the ungodly" (verse 7). He goes on to say, "The earth and the works that are done on it will be exposed" (verse 10).

In wrestling with this passage, one pastor recently concluded, "There is virtually no continuity between the present and the new creation. The new creation is truly new. The old passes away; it is burned up and dissolved." Like this pastor many have tended to see in that last sentence (verse 10) more than what's there, a misunderstanding fueled in part by a questionable translation.

Let me explain.

In the King James Version, this verse reads, "The earth…and the works that are therein shall be *burned up.*" The same "burned up" phrase appears in some modern English versions rooted in the King James tradition. New Testament scholar Thomas Schreiner points out that, indeed, "some Greek manuscripts have this wording (Greek *kataka setai*)" but "the earliest and most reliable manuscripts" have a different Greek phrase, *heureth setai,* carrying the idea of being "found" or "found out."[7] This is what's represented in other English versions, such as these examples:

- "The earth and the works that are done on it *will be exposed.*" (ESV)
- "The earth and everything in it *will be laid bare.*" (NIV)

These translations indicate, not the obliteration of the earth, but rather a type of purging. Notice, too, that the earthly destruction mentioned in 2 Peter 3:6 (from the Flood in Noah's day) is cleansing rather than annihilating.

Schreiner then looks at the bigger picture:

Scholars have debated whether the NT speaks of an annihilation of the present cosmos and the creation of a new universe, or whether it indicates the transformation of the present cosmos, including the earth. The latter seems more likely in light of: (1) the preferred reading of this passage…; (2) Rom. 8:18–25; (3) many OT prophecies about the renewal of the earth; (4) Christ's resurrection body being in continuity with his earthly body; and (5) the fact that Christ's resurrection body is a pattern for the resurrection bodies of Christians (1 Cor. 15:12–58). God seems always to renew, not destroy and recreate, parts of his creation that are marred by sin.[8]

The Romans passage referred to in the previous quote speaks explicitly about all of creation waiting for its ultimate liberation:

The creation waits with eager longing for the revealing of the sons of God. For the creation was subjected to futility, not willingly, but because of him who subjected it, in hope that the creation itself will be set free from its bondage to decay and obtain the freedom of the glory of the children of God. (8:19–21)

God doesn't plan to utterly destroy this present world and build a brand-new world from scratch. Instead he plans a radical renovation project for the world we live in today. The Bible never says that everything will be burned up and replaced. Rather, it says that everything will be purged with fire and restored. God won't destroy everything that now exists, but he will destroy all the corruption, brokenness, and chaos we see in our world, purging from it everything that is impure and sinful.

God's Evacuation Plan?

Matthew 24:37–41 is another passage some use to justify an escapist theology, approaching this world with a "Why shine the brass on a sinking ship?" attitude. In this passage Jesus likens "the coming of the Son of Man" to the time of Noah, when people "were unaware until the flood came and *swept them all away*." Then Jesus gives two brief pictures of the effect of his coming: "Two men will be in the field; *one will be taken and one left*. Two women will be grinding at the mill; *one will be taken and one left*."

These verses have been employed to support the idea that God will one day evacuate, or rapture, all the righteous people, leaving behind an evil world destined for annihilation. Therefore, the thinking goes, Christians should focus exclusively on seeking to rescue lost souls rather than waste time trying to fix things that are broken in this doomed world. This perspective is evidenced in a comment I read not long ago from a well-known Bible teacher: "Evangelism is the *one* reason God's people are still on earth."

But a closer look at the context reveals that in those pictures Jesus gave of men in the field and women at the mill, those left behind are the righteous rather than the unrighteous. Like the people in Noah's day who were swept away, leaving behind Noah and his family to rebuild the world, so the unrighteous are taken while the righteous are left behind. Why? Because this world belongs to God, and he's in the process of gaining it all back, not giving it all up.

When it comes to this world's future, God will follow the same pattern he engineered in Noah's day, when he washed away everything that was perverse and wicked but did not obliterate everything. God will not annihilate the cosmos; he'll renew, redeem, and resurrect it. As Randy Alcorn writes, "We will be the same people made new and we will live on the same Earth made new."[9]

Moreover, the comparison between the floodwaters in Noah's day and the fire that Peter wrote about is significant. The wicked things that are swept away by water can grow back (as happened in Noah's time). But the wicked things burned up by fire can *never* come back. The burning-away effect of fire is permanent; the sweeping-away effect of water isn't. Fire, in this case, is better than flood.

Total Redemption

One thing all of this means is that God intends to bring redemption into every arena where sin has brought corruption—and that's everywhere! As the beloved Christmas hymn "Joy to the World" puts it:

> He comes to make his blessings flow
> Far as the curse is found.

In these remarkable lines we broadcast in song a gospel as large as the universe itself. The blessings of redemption flow as far as the curse is found. This hymn reminds us that the gospel is good news to a world that has, in every imaginable way, been twisted away from the intention of the Creator's design by the powers of sin and death but that God, in Christ, is putting it back into shape.

Because God created peoples, places, and things, and because sin has corrupted peoples, places, and things, God intends to redeem peoples, places, and things. In Christ, God intends to redeem not only individuals but also neighborhoods, schools, and workplaces. He intends to redeem not only environmentalists but also the environment, not just lawyers but also the law, not simply government officials but also government itself (see Isaiah 9:6–7). His goal is to transform every cultural sphere, from art and education to commerce and communication—everything! His mission is to redeem, renew, and regenerate all that is twisted and corrupt, broken and crusted over with sin.

Furthermore, this is a mission God will never abort. He refuses to quit until he has renewed every last inch of his good creation that has been contaminated by evil. "Behold, I am making *all things* new" (Revelation 21:5). The apostle Paul says that God is using the power of Christ's cross to "reconcile to himself *all* things, whether on earth or in heaven" (Colossians 1:20). He speaks of God's "plan for the fullness of time, to unite *all things* in him [Christ], things in heaven and things on earth" (Ephesians 1:10).

Theologian Cornelius Plantinga notes the comprehensiveness of it all: "In a thousand ways, God will gather what's scattered, rebuild what's broken, restore what has been emptied out by centuries of waste and fraud. In a thousand ways, God will put right what's wrong with his glorious creation."[10]

God promises nothing short of *total cosmic renewal.* Our confident anticipation of that renewal—our living hope of it—triggers and sustains our excitement and motivation for making a difference by living unfashionable lives. It links us with something so grand and glorious that it easily exposes the flimsy lie behind mere fashionability.

Let's discover more of this thrilling dynamic we can look forward to.

Redeemed to Renew

> We can love this world because it is God's, and it will
> be healed, becoming at last what God intended from
> the beginning. We are not merely passing through
> this world and this life. We are shaping the building
> blocks of eternity.
>
> —PAUL MARSHALL

●●●●●●

TO ME THE MOST STARTLING ASPECT of God's mission is that he has called fallible people like you and me to take part in carrying out his glorious work of revitalization. He could, of course, do this work without our help. But the fact that he has chosen to use *our* heads, *our* hearts, and *our* hands to do his work—that he even calls us his "body"—ought to both humble us and rouse us to action. In redeeming us, God doesn't simply rescue us *from* our sin; he also rescues us *to* do something—to take up again the assignment we were created for in the first place: the cultural mandate. We're to be doing what God originally called us to do, namely, develop the world around us to the glory of God. We've been redeemed by God to become agents of renewal.

What Jesus Did—and Does

One afternoon not long ago I was having a conversation with a good friend named Mark. We were sitting in a hotel room discussing whether Christians have been enlisted by God to bring about renewal in every cultural arena. Mark was apprehensive about that idea simply because he believed Christians have *one* primary responsibility— evangelism. And if Christians get too involved in seeking to renew our culture, they will become distracted from their principal task. Plus, he added, nowhere in the New Testament are Christians explicitly commanded to be involved in the transformation of things like art or science or education.

It was a good and lively conversation.

My response to Mark had three parts.

First, I explained that we don't need an explicit command in the New Testament to be engaged in the renewal of culture, because the cultural mandate given to Adam still applies. Nowhere does the New Testament abrogate it. The Fall makes it more of a challenge, but it doesn't cancel the order. As we saw in the last chapter, we're still called to be creational caretakers and cultural developers. It's just that now we have to do it by the "sweat of [our] face" among "thorns and thistles" (Genesis 3:18–19).

Second, this means that, while evangelism remains a priority, the salvation of individuals isn't the church's only mission. Churches are designed by God to be instruments of renewal in the world, renewing not only individual lives but also cultural forms and structures, helping to make straight all that is crooked in our world.

My third point to Mark was this: Christians are called to follow Jesus, to go where he's going and to do what he's doing. This is what it means to be his disciple. And the New Testament clearly teaches that Jesus intends to bring about the restoration of *all things*—he's working in the direction of total transformation. Knowing that this is what Jesus is doing and where he's going, Christians are disobedient to the degree that they refuse to follow him in these ways. It's the chief business of every true disciple to be working toward the same end Christ is working toward. The alternative would clearly be sinful non-compliance—thumbing our noses at God's plan.

Looking again at the Lord's Prayer and its reminder that God's ultimate goal is to make earth like heaven raises a question: what's going on in heaven that God intends to bring here on earth? Well, whatever else the Bible might have to say about the current state of affairs in heaven, the Lord's Prayer teaches us that it's an environment—a culture, more accurately—where God's name is perfectly hallowed and his will perfectly done. Obviously this is by no means the situation on earth at the present time, but Jesus foresees the time when the perfect doing of God's will and the perfect hallowing of God's name will be as true on earth as it is in heaven. And contrary to what many have come to believe, this process of transformation does not *begin* when Christ returns.

With Christ's first coming, God began the process of reversing the curse of sin and redeeming all things. In Christ, God was moving in a new way. All of Jesus's ministry—the words he spoke, the miracles he performed—showed that there was a new order in town: God's order. When Jesus healed the diseased, raised the dead, and forgave the desperate, he did so to show that with the arrival of God in the flesh came the restoration of the way God intended things to be.

Tim Keller observes that Christ's miracles were not the *suspension* of the natural order but the *restoration* of the natural order. They were a reminder of what once was, prior to the Fall, and a preview of what will eventually be a universal reality once again—a world of peace and justice without death, disease, or conflict.

In his book *This Beautiful Mess,* Rick McKinley describes his response to the death of a friend:

> I went to the graveside with his family to lead the memorial. The whole time there in the graveyard we felt the sting of death. The awful mess of grief and rage and unfairness was right there under our feet. I hated it. But no one dies in the kingdom of God. It is in the kingdom of Satan, our enemy, where death reigns. A pastor friend of mine told me that as

he was preparing for a funeral once, he decided to go
through the Gospels to see how Jesus dealt with funerals.
What he discovered was that Jesus did not care for them
much. Every one He went to He raised the person from
the dead. Jesus doesn't do funerals, not even his own.[1]

The resurrection of Jesus is the greatest proof of God's intention
to revitalize this broken cosmos. Jesus's rising from the dead was "just
the beginning of the saving, renewing, resurrecting work of God that
will have its climax in the restoration of the entire cosmos," as K. Scott
Oliphint and Sinclair Ferguson remind us.[2] The bodily resurrection of
Jesus "was the first bit of material order to be redeemed and transfigured," writes John Stott. "It is the divine pledge that the rest will be
redeemed and transfigured one day."[3] Christ's resurrection is both the
model and the means for our resurrection—and the guarantee that
he will finish what he started.

The day will come when Christ returns and *completes* this process
of transformation (read Revelation 21, for instance). Psalm 96:11–13
gives us a poetic glimpse of what will happen when Jesus returns to
rule the earth:

Let the heavens be glad, and let the earth rejoice;
     let the sea roar, and all that fills it;
     let the field exult, and everything in it!
Then shall all the trees of the forest sing for joy
     before the LORD, for he comes,
     for he comes to [rule] the earth.
He will [rule] the world in righteousness,
     and the peoples in his faithfulness.

For those who have found forgiveness of sins in Christ, there will
one day be no more sickness, no more death, no more tears, no more
division, no more tension. For the pardoned children of God, there

will be complete harmony. We'll work and worship in a perfectly renewed earth without the interference of sin. We who believe the gospel will enjoy sinless hearts and minds along with disease-free bodies. All that causes us pain and discomfort will be destroyed, and we will live forever. We'll finally be able, as John Piper says, "to enjoy what is most enjoyable with unbounded energy and passion forever."[4]

Making the Crooked Straight

In the meantime—the time between Christ's first and second comings—we, the people of God, have been commissioned to serve as God's agents of renewal, with our own resurrection serving as the pattern for the resurrection of all creation.

This is behind Jesus's commissioning of all his transformed followers: "Go and make disciples of all nations, baptizing them in the name of the Father and of the Son and of the Holy Spirit, and teaching them to obey everything I have commanded you. And surely I am with you always, to the very end of the age" (Matthew 28:19–20, NIV). Commenting on these verses, theologian John Frame says:

> You see how comprehensive that is? The Great Commission tells us not only to tell people the gospel and get them baptized, but also to teach them to obey everything Jesus has commanded us. Everything. The gospel creates new people, people radically committed to Christ in every area of their lives. People like these will change the world. They will fill and rule the earth to the glory of Jesus. They will plant churches, establish godly families, and will also plant godly hospitals, schools, arts, and sciences.[5]

The Great Commission instructs us to bring every part of our lives and every part of our world under the lordship of Christ. When we do, we bring the renewing power of God's reign and rule on earth as it is in heaven.

God's ultimate purpose for Christians is not to bring them out of this world and into heaven but to use them to bring heaven into this world. As we hallow God's name and do God's will in how we think, feel, and act—even when it means being unfashionable—the power of Christ's resurrection flows through us, and as a result we bring heaven's culture to earth; we give people a foretaste of what's to come. In this manner we continue the work Christ began and will one day complete.

Michael Wittmer describes this process vividly:

> Just as sin began with individuals and rippled out to contami-
> nate the entire world, so grace begins with individuals and
> ripples out to redeem the rest of creation. We humans are the
> bull's-eye of God's grace, the target of his redemption. But
> though salvation begins with us, the God who redeems us
> does not want us to keep redemption to ourselves.[6]

God wants us to join him in his work of renewing people, places, and things. He wants Christians to renew their cultures to the honor and glory of God. God wants those he's redeemed to work at trans-forming this broken world and all its broken structures—families, churches, governments, businesses—in a way that reflects an answer to the Lord's Prayer: "Your kingdom come, your will be done, on earth as it is in heaven" (Matthew 6:10). We're to fill every aspect of the earth with the knowledge of God, our Creator and Redeemer.

You might be wondering, *But what about cultural forms that are severely warped and deformed? For example, the pornography industry. Is there anything renewable about that perverse structure?*

That's a great question. No, the depraved industry of pornogra-phy is not renewable. But here's the point: the pornography industry is built on an *ethical misuse* (caused by the Fall) of something God created as good, namely sex. We redirect (redeem) sex away from this ethical misuse when we recover and celebrate God's original intention for it. When we replace sexual exploitation with beautiful,

God-ordained human intimacy enjoyed between husband and wife, we do our part to make the crooked course of sexual misuse straight.

Our mission involves both evangelism and cultural renewal. This is true because God exercises his dominion both through *saving* grace (the means by which he converts people, raising them from spiritual death to spiritual life in Christ) and *common* grace (the goodness he shows to *all* people, Christians and non-Christians). Jesus refers to common grace in Matthew 5:45: "Your Father...makes his sun rise on the evil and on the good, and sends rain on the just and on the unjust." By his common grace God upholds the created order and restrains evil so that the effects of the Fall aren't as bad as they would otherwise be. So when God's people devote themselves to showing good to all by developing and advancing such created goods as medicine, technology, art, and education and by upholding created institutions such as marriage and the family, and by fixing things in this world that are broken because of the Fall—they're serving as mediators of God's common grace.

Therefore, the mission of the church is spiritual *and* physical, individual *and* cultural. God wants us to involve ourselves in the rehabilitation of hearts *and* houses, souls *and* society. We're to care about the renewal of both people and the environment. This requires word *and* deed, proclamation *and* demonstration. God is renewing human hearts and recreating all things through his church. This is our mission to the world.

No Utopia Now

To be sure, a transformational approach to culture does not assume an unrealistic optimism about what's possible in our fallen world. Because the world will remain sinful until Christ returns, we know we can never achieve any utopia here and now. Heaven on earth will become a universal reality only when Christ comes back.

In this regard it's been helpful for me to understand the distinction Abraham Kuyper made between "persuasion" and "coercion." For Kuyper, persuasion is the Christian's role and responsibility toward culture here and now—seeking to *influence* every sphere of society (such as the family, government, education) for Christ and bringing the standards of God's Word to bear on every dimension of human culture. Coercion, on the other hand, is the role and responsibility of Christ, not Christians. Jesus alone possesses the right and power to "coerce," or force, culture in a Godward direction, and this is a right he will fully exercise only when he returns to make "all things new" (Revelation 21:5). Understanding the difference between persuasion and coercion—between our role and Christ's role—helps us serve God with realistic expectations.[7]

Of course there has always been considerable (and somewhat distracting) debate on whether before Christ returns, things will get markedly worse, get markedly better, or just go on about the same. The answer to that is God's business, not ours. We're told to plant and water; God alone controls the results.

Our task as faithful disciples is proclaimed by the Welsh poet Ethelwyn Wetherald:

> My orders are to fight;
> Then if I bleed, or fail,
> Or strongly win, what matters it?
> God only doth prevail.
> The servant craveth naught
> Except to serve with might.
> I was not told to win or lose—
> My orders are to fight.[8]

What we do know is that many Christians throughout the ages have sought cultural transformation, and in so doing they've had a huge impact on the world. One of them was the English politician William Wilberforce, whose conversion to Christianity impelled him to fight against the slave trade throughout the British Empire. He did this for decades, paving the way for the abolition of slavery and the reformation of morals in England. He was truly a man who changed his times. When Christians take the cultural mandate seriously, real change for the better can and has happened. No Christian has ever "turned earth into heaven, or the world into the church," says John Frame. "And sometimes they have made tragic mistakes. But they have also done a great deal of good."[9]

The good news is that Christ not only began the process but also will complete it. And by his Spirit he now empowers us to carry on his work. Led by Christ and empowered by the Holy Spirit, we thus have all we need for our present task. In saving us God has fully equipped us to carry out the cultural mandate he originally entrusted to us.

What About Political Involvement?

When it comes to transforming culture, many Christians think exclusively of political activism. I fully agree that Christians need to be involved in the political process; as I've argued, Christians are to bring the standards of God's Word to bear on *every* cultural sphere, politics included.

But political activism isn't the only thing—definitely not the *main* thing—God had in mind when he issued the cultural mandate to mankind. Nor is politics a particularly strategic arena for cultural renewal, as theologian Vern Poythress writes:

> Bible-believing Christians have not achieved much in politics because they have not devoted themselves to the larger arena of cultural conflict. Politics mostly follows culture rather than leading it…. A temporary victory in the voting booth does not reverse a downward moral trend driven by cultural gatekeepers in news media, entertainment, art, and education. Politics is not a cure-all.[10]

After decades of political activism on the part of evangelical Christians, we're beginning to understand that the dynamics of cultural change differ radically from political mobilization. Even political insiders recognize that years of political effort on behalf of evangelical Christians have generated little cultural gain. In a recent article entitled "Religious Right, R.I.P.," columnist Cal Thomas, himself an evangelical Christian, wrote, "Thirty years of trying to use government to stop abortion, preserve opposite-sex marriage, improve television and movie content and transform culture into the conservative Evangelical image has failed."[11] American culture continues its steep moral and cultural decline into hedonism and materialism. Why? As Richard John Neuhaus observes, "Christianity in America is not challenging the 'habits of the heart' and 'habits of the mind' that dominate American culture."[12]

For a long time now, I've been convinced that what happens in New York (finance), Hollywood (entertainment), Silicon Valley (technology), and Miami (fashion) has a far greater impact on how our culture thinks about reality than what happens in Washington DC (politics). It's superimportant for us to understand that politics are reflective, not directive. That is, the political arena is the place where policies are made that *reflect* the values of our culture—the habits of heart and mind—that are being shaped by these other, more strategic arenas. As the Scottish politician Andrew Fletcher said, "Let me write the songs of a nation; I don't care who writes its laws."

Why Waste Time?

Since God is on a mission to transform this present world into the world to come, and since he's using his transformed people to do it, our commitment to living unfashionably has cosmic implications. The difference God has equipped us to make is neither small nor insignificant; God has created us to live for something that will never die. Our call to live against the world for the world—to live unfashionably—

bears the power to effect real, lasting change to peoples, places, and things both now and forever.

So why waste time and energy living for here-today-gone-tomorrow trends when we can live for something that will go on and on and on?

Ultimately the power of Christianity is diminished when we turn it into our individual quest to go to heaven. Christianity is about so much more. The gospel reveals God's intention to transform this broken world, to miraculously make "everything sad come untrue." It triumphantly proclaims his power to undo everything evil, straighten out all that's crooked, and correct every injustice. In Jesus, God is at work regaining, restoring, and extending what Adam forfeited by his disobedience. The last Adam achieves for us no less than what the first Adam enjoyed, and much more. We won't simply go back to Eden; we'll enjoy a whole new incorruptible world.

The exciting good news is that Christ is presently carrying out this cosmic renovation through those who have been reconciled to God through his atoning work on the cross. With the death and resurrection of Jesus Christ, God commenced a counterattack to reclaim his rightful territory, and Christians are his soldiers in that continuing battle. God has called Christians to play a role by celebrating what's good and true and beautiful, working for change in what isn't, and looking forward in hope to God's redemption of all things.

You can become a part of God's unstoppable reclamation project by being united to Christ and following him, that is, by living unfashionably. And as we continue exploring what this future truly holds, I believe you'll conclude without a doubt that it's worth living for—and dying for.

Presence of the Future

> Another world is possible.... Another world is
> necessary.... Another world is already here.
>
> —SHANE CLAIBORNE

✱✱✱✱✱✱

ONE OF THE PRIMARY BIBLICAL DESCRIPTIONS of those who know God
is that we are citizens in God's kingdom. As Christians fully embrace
our calling to be unfashionable, we'll need to gain a deeper understanding of what this kingdom is and what it means to be a part of it.

Such an understanding is urgently needed. The church at the
beginning of the twenty-first century faces an unparalleled identity
crisis. Unfortunately, ongoing reappraisals of the church's role in culture, which include analyses of contemporary trends and how the
church should respond, have so far generated mostly confusion and
heated debates. The proposed solutions vary widely, and no consensus has emerged.

The correct solution, I believe, lies in the church's ability to recover
a biblically defined understanding of who we are, where we come
from, and where we're headed. Unless we answer these identity questions, we'll never know how we should then live, and we'll continue
to surrender our transformational influence in this world. When we
don't have a clear sense of what makes us different, we lose our ability
to make a difference.

That's why I want to take a closer look now at what it means to
be a citizen of God's kingdom.

Divinely Relocated

If you're a Christian, you've been objectively transferred by God from the realm of spiritual death to the realm of spiritual life—from a domain where sin and death rule to a kingdom where God rules. The apostle Paul explains it this way: "He has delivered us from the domain of darkness and transferred us to the kingdom of his beloved Son, in whom we have redemption, the forgiveness of sins" (Colossians 1:13–14).

Your citizenship has changed. You're a subject of a new Ruler. This external relocation to a new kingdom governed by King Jesus inevitably leads to, and is inseparable from, an internal revolution. Paul explains this relationship between the external and the internal:

> We were buried…with him by baptism into death, in order that, just as Christ was raised from the dead by the glory of the Father, we too might walk in newness of life.
>
> For if we have been united with him in a death like his, we shall certainly be united with him in a resurrection like his. We know that our old self was crucified with him in order that the body of sin might be brought to nothing, so that we would no longer be enslaved to sin. (Romans 6:4–6)

For those who are Christians—those who have come under the reign and rule of King Jesus—sin no longer has mastery over them or dominion in them. They are no longer slaves to sin.

To be sure, Christians still struggle with sin, because even though sin has already been dethroned, it hasn't yet been destroyed. But as John Murray says, "It is one thing for the enemy to occupy the capital; it is another for his defeated hosts to harass the garrisons of the Kingdom."[1] Sin still remains in us, but it doesn't reign over us. King Jesus now occupies the throne in our souls, with dominion in us and mastery over us. Meanwhile, remaining sin continues its ruthless assaults, employing a guerrilla warfare type of strategy as it continually resists God's new governing authority in and over us.

But even though sin's harassment is real and deeply felt, the Bible wants Christians to know we're fundamentally different than we used to be. This external relocation, with its accompanying internal revolution, means that we're new creatures with new natures—"the old has gone, the new has come!" (2 Corinthians 5:17, NIV).

Your core has been radically changed. Your disposition, your desires, and your direction have been radically adjusted—you've been raised to newness of life. This newness expresses itself in new thoughts, new desires, and new behavior. You'll think differently, feel differently, live differently.

This is why, as I mentioned earlier, we're to operate according to a different standard, with different goals and motivations and an altogether different perspective on money, lifestyle, and relationships. Our priorities and pursuits and passions—everything is to be different. It makes no sense to live according to the old ways when we've become new. The New Testament contains exhortation after exhortation for Christians to become what they are, to live out practically what they already are positionally: citizens in the kingdom of God.

But in order for citizens in God's kingdom to do this, they need to know more about this kingdom, this new land they've been transferred to.

The Kingdom of God: What Is It?

The Bible has so much to say about the kingdom of God that it's surprising many Christians are unable to give a concise and biblically informed description of it. It's even more surprising when you remember Jesus's exhortation to "seek first the kingdom of God" (Matthew 6:33), showing the inseparable relationship between God's kingdom and the Christian life. According to Jesus it's impossible that one could properly understand the practical nature of living the Christian life, and especially our call as Christians to make a difference in this world by being different, without properly understanding the nature of our citizenship in God's kingdom. One cannot be a faithful follower of Christ the King without being a faithful citizen in his kingdom and knowing what that entails.

So what is the kingdom of God?

Sinclair Ferguson defines the kingdom as "the rule and reign of God, the expression of his gracious sovereign will. To belong to the kingdom of God is to belong to the people among whom the reign of God has already begun."[2] George Eldon Ladd defines the kingdom as "the realm in which God's reign may be experienced."[3] Simply put, the kingdom of God is a kingdom where God's appointed King—Jesus—is presently reigning in and through the lives of his people, accomplishing his will "on earth as it is in heaven" (Matthew 6:10).

The presence and purpose of God's kingdom undergird the teaching of the whole Bible, exhibiting God's plan—past, present, and future—for this world. There's no shortage of kingdom-mindedness among Scripture's authors. For instance, David prays, "Yours is the *kingdom*, O LORD, and you are exalted as head above all" (1 Chronicles 29:11). He rejoices over that fact in Psalm 103:19: "The LORD has established his throne in heaven, and his *kingdom* rules over all" (NIV).

This kingdom was shown, even in the Old Testament, to be the exalted identity for the people of God, as seen in the heavenly visions given to Daniel:

> The *kingdom* and the dominion
> and the greatness of the kingdoms under the whole
> heaven
> shall be given to the people of the saints of the Most
> High;
> *their kingdom shall be an everlasting kingdom,*
> and all dominions shall serve and obey them.
> (Daniel 7:27)

In the New Testament the first recorded sermons of both John the Baptist and Jesus are identical kingdom proclamations: "Repent, for the *kingdom* of heaven is at hand" (Matthew 3:2; 4:17). The kingdom continued to be a recurring emphasis in the Lord's teachings throughout his earthly ministry. And later, in the days between his resurrection and his ascension, Jesus appeared to his disciples, "speaking about the *kingdom* of God" (Acts 1:3).

In Acts we see how Philip the evangelist "preached good news about the *kingdom* of God and the name of Jesus Christ" (Acts 8:12). And we hear the apostle Paul testifying, "I have gone about proclaiming the *kingdom*" (20:25). The book of Acts ends with Paul in Rome, "proclaiming the *kingdom* of God and teaching about the Lord Jesus Christ with all boldness" (28:31).

Further in the New Testament, the eternal dimensions of this kingdom are emphasized. The author of Hebrews exhorts us, "Let us be grateful for receiving a *kingdom* that cannot be shaken." James reminds us that God's people are "heirs of the kingdom." And Peter looks forward to our "entrance into the eternal *kingdom* of our Lord and Savior Jesus Christ" (Hebrews 12:28; James 2:5; 2 Peter 1:11).

The most exhaustive description of God's kingdom, though, is given to us by Jesus in the Sermon on the Mount (Matthew 5–7), where he shows the kingdom of God to be central to his teaching and to all of the Christian life. Throughout this sermon Jesus forthrightly shows what kingdom living in a fallen world looks like, as the kingdom shapes our experience here and now.

John Stott, in his book *Christian Counter-Culture,* explores Jesus's teaching here. He outlines how God's kingdom is a radical departure from the values and ways of this world—in our personal character (Matthew 5:3–12), influence (5:13–16), virtue (5:17–48), piety (6:1–18), ambitions (6:19–34), relationships (7:1–20), and commitments (7:21–27). Stott contends that the key verse in Christ's sermon is 6:8, where Jesus says, "Do not be like them." That verse recalls God's instruction to Israel in Leviticus 18:3: "You shall not do as they do."

Contrary to what we hear these days from some Christian leaders, no observation could be more condemning to the Christian than for a non-Christian to say, "You're no different than I am."

For Jesus, what it means to be a Christian cannot be divorced from an understanding of the kingdom of God.

Remember Pontius Pilate's conversation with Jesus about his kingdom? Under Pilate's questioning, Jesus responded, "My kingdom is not of this world" (John 18:36). What did that mean? Jesus meant that the kingdom of God is unlike any kingdom this world has ever known: it has a different King, who rules according to different standards for different reasons. Compared to any other kingdom in this world, God's kingdom and its ways seem upside-down, backward, absurd—which is why those who follow Jesus are certain to be unfashionable.

A closer look at God's strange kingdom will inescapably whet our appetites for the future.

Expanding It

In the Old Testament, God's kingdom was largely limited to the people and land of Israel; for the most part it was expressed and exhibited locally and nationally. In the New Testament, God's kingdom is extended to all peoples and all lands, and it begins to be expressed and exhibited universally and internationally.

This expansion of the kingdom happens in three stages: inauguration, continuation, and consummation.[4]

The Kingdom's Inauguration
With the arrival of King Jesus to this earth, God's kingdom began its expansion into international and universal dimensions.

To be sure, Jesus Christ had always been Lord over all creation. "By him all things were created... And he is before all things, and in him all things hold together" (Colossians 1:16–17). Since the dawn of time, there has never been a moment when the Lord hasn't reigned over all he has made. But God's reign was demonstrated in new and dramatic ways when Jesus brought it from heaven to earth in a paradigm-shattering manner.

Previously "he looked down from his holy height; from heaven the LORD looked at the earth" (Psalm 102:19). That is, prior to the incarnation the Lord ruled from afar (although he has always acted providentially on the earth). But then Jesus came and announced, "The time is fulfilled, and the *kingdom* of God is *at hand*" (Mark 1:15). The time had come; God's kingdom was right here with us: "The Word became flesh and dwelt among us, and we have seen his glory, glory as of the only Son from the Father, full of grace and truth" (John 1:14). Here was God's kingdom earthed.

All of Jesus's words and deeds demonstrated that God's reign had invaded this fallen world to make all things new. A new day had dawned. When Jesus cast out demons, he did so to show God's power over evil. When he healed the sick and raised the dead, he showed that with the arrival of God's kingdom came redemption and cleansing, healing and forgiveness. New life was given; health was restored. In the imagery of C. S. Lewis's Narnia, the grip of an unending winter was finally broken. The inauguration of God's kingdom through Jesus began the great reversal—repealing the curse of sin and death, ensuring that God had begun the process of renewing all things.

The Kingdom's Continuation

The continuation stage of the kingdom of God is where we are now—a stage marked by tension between present and future. We're in the period of redemptive history often referred to as "already and not yet." The kingdom is already here in true form, but it is not yet in its full form. It is present in its beginnings but still future in its fullness.

In this stage God continues his process of reversing the curse of sin and renewing all things through his citizens as he expands his kingdom by building his church. The evidence of God's kingdom in this stage is not the final removal of death and disease but rather the transformation of human lives.

This transformation is possible because our King is with us. "Jesus continues to be our Prophet, Priest, and King," as Richard Pratt explains. "As our Prophet he teaches through the faithful preaching of the Word (2 Peter 3:2). As our Priest he intercedes on our behalf before the throne of grace. As our King he leads us into battle, protecting and providing for our needs."[5]

In this stage our King also happens to be the Great Evangelist, calling men and women to himself, setting them apart as "unfashionable," then sending them out into the world to make his invisible kingdom visible. This happens as we, in and under the Holy Spirit's power, live what one theologian calls "the cruciformed life"—reaching up to God and reaching out to people so that our lives form the posture of the cross.

God's kingdom in this stage is not only continuing to expand *through* us but also continuing to expand *in* us. God is at work to renew our hearts and minds, reversing the effects of sin in our lives and reordering our priorities. So while we're not yet what we will be, we're also no longer what we used to be. As Maurice Roberts says, "We are at present in a state of transition. God hasn't finished his work in us as yet. But when God's work concerning us is complete, we shall be all that we ought to be and all that we now long to be."[6]

We're like Israel during her wilderness wanderings—we've left Egypt but haven't yet entered the Promised Land.

The Kingdom's Consummation

The third stage, the kingdom's consummation, will take place when Jesus comes back and the process of reversing the curse of sin and recreating all things is completed (see 1 Corinthians 15:51–58). As we've seen, when our King returns, there will be no more sickness, no more death, no more tears, no more division, no more tension. The peace on earth that the angels announced the night Christ was born will become a universal actuality. God's cosmic rescue mission will be complete. The fraying fabric of our fallen world will be fully and perfectly rewoven. Everything and everyone "in Christ" will live in perfect harmony. *Shalom* will rule.

Isaiah pictures it this way:

The wolf shall dwell with the lamb,
    and the leopard shall lie down with the young goat,
and the calf and the lion and the fattened calf together;
    and a little child shall lead them.
The cow and the bear shall graze;
    their young shall lie down together;
    and the lion shall eat straw like the ox.
The nursing child shall play over the hole of the cobra,
    and the weaned child shall put his hand on the adder's den.
They shall not hurt or destroy
    in all my holy mountain;
for the earth shall be full of the knowledge of the LORD
    as the waters cover the sea. (11:6–9)

In that day every knee will bow and every tongue confess that Jesus Christ is King over all. The new heavens and the new earth will be set up, their glory on full display, free of imperfections.

In his first coming Jesus inaugurated his kingdom in the world. He's already ruling and reigning, he has defeated (but not yet destroyed) the god of this age, and he is seated on his throne at the right hand of the Father. Yet the resistance remains; the combat carries on. In his second coming he'll consummate his kingdom, not simply defeating and dethroning every enemy, but destroying them.

The kingdom in its consummation stage will be a fully visible reality, whereas now, in its continuation stage, it's only partially visible. God's kingdom manifests itself here and now through the transformed lives of his people and the building of his church, but this manifestation is both incomplete and imperfect, because the kingdom's citizens are both incomplete and imperfect.

In that future consummation stage, the kingdom will transform people outwardly as well as inwardly, giving them new bodies in the likeness of the resurrected Christ. Meanwhile, in its continuation stage, the kingdom transforms people inwardly, giving them new hearts and making them alive with Christ. So while we're *already* a genuinely new creation, we're *not yet* a totally new creation.

Those who are citizens in God's kingdom have much to look forward to. For those who have been brought under the reign and rule of King Jesus, the best is yet to come!

Because we're citizens of a different kingdom ruled by a different King, Christians will be different people. We're the people of the future, formed by the past, and living in the present. This should be all the evidence we need to be convinced that being unfashionable—living against the world for the world—is not simply what we're to do; it's *who we are.*

And *who we are* is inescapably linked with our deepest assumptions and perceptions about where we're headed.

Journeying To

Taking a road trip without a clear understanding of the destination is likely to lead to a difficult and frustrating journey. That's why God's people throughout the Bible are given glimpses of their final destination. We're given a road map telling us where we're going and how to get there. Having a kingdom mind-set means understanding that road map. In fact, the descriptions in the Bible concerning our destination (the consummation of the kingdom) are just as physical and tangible as the descriptions in the Bible of *how* we're to get there (the continuation of the kingdom).

Not long ago I was listening to an excellent message by an excellent preacher on how we're to live radically for Jesus. He gave a moving exhortation on how we're to manage that journey—how we're to invest our daily energy for Christ's sake as citizens of God's kingdom. He described the nature of radical Christian living in tangible, practical ways. I sat there with mental pictures in my head that I could almost touch and taste. It was *that* practical, *that* physically descriptive. But when he later began describing why it is important to live radically for Jesus and where it will eventually lead us (our destination), his descriptions became ethereal. He ended by basically saying, "Living this way will lead you to the place where you'll be eternally satisfied in the glory of God."

Now, it's true that every genuine follower of Christ ought to be motivated to see the glory of God. But I left thinking, *What does that look like? feel like? smell like?* I was left hanging. The preacher had done a remarkable job of describing the physical, tangible nature of the continuation stage of the kingdom—how to live as a kingdom citizen in a fallen world here and now. But he'd missed the mark in explaining the physical, tangible nature of where we're headed—the consummation stage of the kingdom. And we need that too for a crucial reason: our *eschatology* (how we understand the consummation of God's kingdom) dramatically affects our *missiology* (what we're to do in the meantime). If we don't have a vivid understanding of what the divine objective is, our mission will lack focus, direction, and purpose. We won't have the sense of identity we desperately need as twenty-first-century pilgrims.

After all, wasn't it Christian's clear vision of the Celestial City in *Pilgrim's Progress* that enabled him to press on and strain forward through all his opposition on the way there? Søren Kierkegaard once said, "You have to define life backwards. You have to start from the end and move towards the present. What's the purpose of life? What's it about? Is it possible to borrow from the end to enrich the now?"

This is why it's helpful for me to think about what's ahead.

Right now we live in what C. S. Lewis called "the shadowlands." Everything now is a pale reflection of what things will one day be like. But when King Jesus returns to consummate his kingdom on earth as it is in heaven, we'll rediscover all the places we used to enjoy, minus the sin, brokenness, and corruption.

I so look forward to that day, returning to God's remade world to see what he's done to all my favorite places. It's hard to imagine how

God could possibly improve on the Swiss Alps, a sunset over the Gulf of Mexico, a clear night with countless stars in the sky, or—my personal favorite—the ocean in all its wonders.

I love the ocean and the beach. I love everything about them—the warm Florida water, the sea breeze blowing through the palms, the calming sound of the waves, the hot sun on my skin. My family and I live just fifteen minutes from the beach, and we like to go as often as we can to sit in the sun and play in the water. I can't wait to experience a perfect new ocean under a more perfect sun.

As we've seen, the Bible teaches that those who know God will one day live in a new, sin-free physical world with new, sin-free physical bodies. We'll have new, sin-free job responsibilities and personal relationships. The Bible speaks about the fact that when Christ comes back to consummate his kingdom on earth as it is in heaven, *all* things we currently experience will not be eliminated but rather made new.

Surprisingly, perhaps the most satisfying thing about this newness we're looking forward to is that, in the deepest sense, what's new will have no sense of strangeness about it. In fact, it all makes up the true home we've always wanted.

Transplants Looking Homeward

Before my wife and I moved back home to South Florida six years ago, we lived in many different places. This means that for the first ten years of our married life, we were transplants wherever we went. Anyone who has moved far from home can testify to the fact that being a transplant can be difficult and uncomfortable. One never really feels quite at home.

When we would come into contact with someone whose family had lived in the same place for generations, we would think how nice it must be to have such deep roots. But then we would begin to reflect on the kingdom of God and how different it is from any home on earth. We would realize afresh that, in God's kingdom, all its citizens have this in common: we're all transplants. None of us was born a citizen in his kingdom. We were born into enemy territory, and each of us was personally sought after by the King, bought by the King's blood, and graciously enrolled by him as citizens in his kingdom. None of us deserves membership in that glorious family, let alone the royal benefits that go with it.

All over the world there are people who right now are being sought by the King. As citizens in his kingdom, we have the privilege of bearing before them the marks of kingdom citizenship and showing them the way out of darkness. The world desperately needs the church to be the church, reflecting the kingdom of God so that those who are lost will know where to turn when their own kingdoms begin to collapse.

One of the reasons Jesus hasn't yet returned to consummate his kingdom is that he's busy seeking new citizens. The only requirement for their becoming a citizen in God's kingdom is to repent of their refusal to bow the knee to King Jesus in humble, glad submission. But all who turn from their sin and turn to Christ in faith take up residence with us in the kingdom of God. And when this happens, their lives will begin to change as they join us in bearing the characteristics of our King.

Yes, opposition will arise from both the outside and the inside. But as hostile forces try to divert us from the narrow road, we'll move forward with confidence, knowing there's a day coming when we'll join heavenly voices in declaring, "The kingdom of the world has become the kingdom of our Lord and of his Christ, and he shall reign forever and ever" (Revelation 11:15).

Where in the World Are Christians?

The church and its gospel throw into question the agenda of the world—all the agendas of the world— and open the world to possibilities of which it has never dared to dream. When the church dares to be different, it models for the world what God calls the world to become.

— RICHARD JOHN NEUHAUS

●●●●●●

BECAUSE GOD IS ON A MISSION to transform this present world into the world to come, and because he's enlisted Christians to join him in this work, the difference we can make in this world is neither small nor insignificant; it's a cosmic difference. Meanwhile, as God's current agents of renewal, our effectiveness depends on our faithfulness to live according to God's standards, as opposed to the standards of this world. Our mission requires us to understand what Jesus meant in John 17 when he prayed that his disciples would be in the world but not of the world.

In the world but not *of* it? How, exactly, do we do that? What should be our approach? What's the proper relationship between the church and the world, between Christ and culture?

There's never been a consensus. Throughout history believers in Christ have approached the culture around them in a variety of ways, including some radically different directions—everything from the simple and solemn Amish to today's pierced, tattooed, "cool" youth pastors. Some have rebuked culture or avoided it at all costs; others have conformed to it, often unwittingly. We've found it easy, as Andy Crouch points out in his book *Culture Making*, to condemn culture, critique culture, copy culture, and consume culture. All too often we are guilty of cocooning, combating, or conforming.

Pointing to something better than these typical postures is the example of Jesus. "Few of us know what it means to actually love the world with the kind of passionate, visionary love that sent Jesus from the heights of holiness into the depths of a sin-sick culture."[1] How do we share in his passion? How do we love the world in a transformative way?

In the World, Not of the World

The Bible makes it clear that Christians need to be people of double listening—listening to both the questions of the world and the answers of the Word. We're responsible to be good interpreters not only of Scripture but also of culture. God calls us to be like the men of Issachar, "who had understanding of the times, to know what Israel ought to do" (1 Chronicles 12:32). Faithfulness to Christ means we cannot afford to leave our culture unexamined. We're called to think long and hard, deep and wide about our times and all the issues surrounding the mission of the church—its proper relationship *to* this world as well as its proper place *in* it.

One helpful word picture here comes from the great nineteenth-century evangelist D. L. Moody. He was once asked to describe what he thought the relationship between the church and the world ought to be. He answered, "The place for the ship is in the sea; but God help the ship if the sea gets into it." We need to avoid being culturally removed—failing to be "in the world," like a ship out of water. We also need to avoid being culturally relaxed—becoming "of the world," like a ship being submerged.

Using Moody's picture, the place for the church is in the world, but God help the church if the world gets into it. Christ has called his followers to be in the world yet distinct from it, to live against the world for the world. The truth is, if you follow Jesus in this way, you will seem "too pagan for your Christian friends and too Christian for your pagan friends."[2]

Avoid Being Culturally Removed

We find the most explicit antithesis between Christians and the world (in the sense of worldliness) in these words from John:

> Do not love the world or anything in the world. If anyone loves the world, the love of the Father is not in him. For everything in the world—the cravings of sinful man, the lust of his eyes and the boasting of what he has and does— comes not from the Father but from the world. The world and its desires pass away, but the man who does the will of God lives forever. (1 John 2:15–17, NIV)

John clearly conveys the sense in which we ought to be separate from the world around us. But this separation is to be *spiritual,* not *spatial.* Spatial separation is wrong; spiritual separation is right.

Surprisingly to some, the Bible never tells Christians to leave the world. On the contrary we're specifically sent to the world. Jesus prayed to the Father concerning his disciples: "As you sent me into the world, so I have sent them into the world" (John 17:18). And also this: "I do not ask that you take them out of the world, but that you keep them from the evil one" (17:15). Jesus didn't invite the world to come to church; he directed the church to go into the world (see Matthew 28). This means every Christian is a missionary. We've been sent by Jesus, the captain of our salvation, into enemy territory to continue the work he began and will one day complete.

Cultural withdrawal, then, isn't an option for followers of Jesus.

In Matthew 5:13–16, Jesus calls us to be "the salt of the earth" and "the light of the world," serving as both a preservative and a lighthouse to the world. But consider this: salt and light have no effect without first *making contact* with something. Salt prevents decay only when it comes into contact with the meat it's meant to preserve. A dark room cannot be lighted until a lamp is brought in and placed where it will shine. Jesus points out the worthlessness of a lamp hidden under a table; for light to be useful, it must be visible to all, like a city on a hill. Like salt and light, we must make contact with the world around us so others see our good deeds and praise our Father in heaven. Withdrawal from this world is therefore not only selfish but also sinful.

One cautionary example of such withdrawal is what happened to Protestant fundamentalism, which began in the early twentieth century as a movement to defend orthodox Christian belief and practice against rising liberalism in the church. Fundamentalists soon became strongly separatist, seeing the main problem not as "in here" (in our sinful nature) but "out there." Cultural retreat was deemed the only way to remain faithful and undefiled; militant separation from the world became the true test of faith.

While working on this book, I had a conversation about fundamentalism with a woman in her sixties. With tears in her eyes, she told me about her strict, cold, Christian upbringing, which taught her that being different meant girls couldn't wear pants, makeup, or jewelry, and guys had to have short hair and be clean-shaven. Guys and girls couldn't swim together in the same pool, movies were strictly off-limits, alcohol was forbidden, and any music other than classical music and hymns was clearly "of the devil." And associating with anyone who broke those rules was a violation of Christian purity.

This woman grew up being told that the church was a tribe, not a mission, and its chief objective was self-preservation from the world, not self-sacrifice for the world. When I explained that this wasn't the kind of difference I was calling for in my book, she was understandably relieved.

The kind of self-righteous and radical withdrawal by Christians this woman described to me isn't nearly as prevalent today as it was in past decades. That's a good thing. But a less obvious form of cultural withdrawal and retreat is gaining momentum.

As I travel to churches around this country, I've noticed a growing trend: traditional places of worship are turning into sprawling campuses—cities within cities. Many churches now have their own restaurants, nightclubs, gymnasiums, bookstores, food courts, cafés, fitness centers, game rooms, and baseball fields. They provide their own sports leagues, exercise programs, and yellow pages. I understand the benefit of some of these things, but when churches provide a substitute activity site for everything under the sun—effectively setting up a parallel universe—we run the risk of abandoning contact with the very world God has commanded us and equipped us to change.

As Andy Crouch points out, "When we copy culture within our own private enclaves, the culture at large remains unchanged."[3] Christians who retreat into a comfortable subculture are bad missionaries— it's that simple.

Centrifugal Force

Remember, making contact is a key to salt's and light's effectiveness. That's why Jesus's command in Matthew 28:19 is that we "go."

His command reflects the impact of the new covenant on the mission of God's people. Under the old covenant, Israel was a nation blessed by God in order to be a blessing to other nations (see Psalm 67), but Israel's function as a community of blessing was primarily (though not exclusively) *centripetal*; instead of Israel going to the nations to give blessing, the nations came to Israel to receive it. Think of the Gentile women Rahab and Ruth, both of whom received the blessing of God by coming into his covenant community.

Under the new covenant, while it's true that blessings await those who enter into the visible church, the church's function as a community of blessing is primarily (though not exclusively) *centrifugal*; the church goes out into the world to bring God's blessing of redemption and renewal to the whole earth.

My friend Trevin often makes the distinction between "sink Christians" and "faucet Christians." Sink Christians, he says, view salvation as something to soak up. It fills the sink, and they soak in the benefits (heaven, peace, Jesus, etc.). Faucet Christians see salvation as something that comes *to* them in order to flow out *through* them to the rest of the world as a blessing to others, as a pipe carries water from its source to a parched land. I like that.

We're called to be "fishers of men" (Matthew 4:19), and we're to be Christ's witnesses "in Jerusalem and in all Judea and Samaria, and *to the end of the earth*" (Acts 1:8). We go out in order to give.

When we operate according to the idea "If we build it, they will come," we fail to take into account this distinct nature of new covenant ministry and mission. Instead we're called to operate with this mind-set: "God is building; therefore we should go."

Renew Where You Are

Martin Luther was once approached by a man who enthusiastically announced that he'd recently become a Christian. Wanting desperately to serve the Lord, he asked Luther, "What should I *do* now?" as if to say, should he become a minister or perhaps a traveling evangelist?

Luther asked him, "What is your work now?"

"I'm a shoemaker."

Much to the cobbler's surprise, Luther replied, "Then make a good shoe and sell it at a fair price."

In becoming Christians we don't need to retreat from the vocational calling we already have. Nor do we need to justify that calling, whatever it is, in terms of its spiritual value or evangelistic usefulness. We simply exercise whatever our calling is with new God-glorifying motives, goals, and standards—and with a renewed commitment to performing our calling with greater excellence and higher objectives.

One way we reflect our Creator is by being creative right where we are with the talents and gifts he has given us. As Paul says, "Each one should remain in the condition in which he was called.... So, brothers, in whatever condition each was called, there let him remain with God" (1 Corinthians 7:20, 24). As we do this, we fulfill our God-given mandate to reform, to beautify our various stations for God's glory.

I once heard Os Guinness speak about what such reform will require. He said the main reason Christians aren't making more of a difference in our world is not that they aren't *where* they should be. There are, in other words, plenty of artists, lawyers, doctors, and business owners who are Christians. Rather, the main reason is that Christians aren't *who* they should be right where they are.

Outwardly there may be no clearly discernible difference between a non-Christian's work and that of a Christian. Many have noted that a transformational approach to culture doesn't mean every human activity practiced by a Christian (designing computers, repairing cars, selling insurance, or whatever) must be obviously and externally different from the same activities practiced by non-Christians. Rather, the difference is found in "the motive, goal, and standard." John Frame writes, "The Christian seeks to change his tires to the glory of God and the non-Christian does not. But that's a difference that couldn't be captured in a photograph. When changing tires, a Christian and non-Christian may look very much alike."[4]

Not only is Christ the Lord of the church; he's also supreme over the family, the arts, the sciences, and human society at large. In the famous words of Abraham Kuyper, "There is not one square inch in the entire domain of our human existence over which Christ, who is Sovereign over all, does not cry, 'Mine!' "

That's why we must not withdraw from the world but rather bring the standards of God's Word to bear on every dimension of human culture. Making a difference for Christ means bringing every area of our lives under his lordship. We must live in passionate devotion to him at all times and in all circumstances. As we do this, God's renewing power is unleashed through us.

So while Christians are to separate from the self-glorifying motives, God-ignoring goals, and subpar work standards of the world (our spiritual separation), we're not to separate from the peoples, places, and things in the world (a spatial separation). We're to be morally and spiritually distinct without being culturally segregated.

In Luke 16:9 Jesus encourages his disciples to match the resourcefulness of worldly people in reaching goals, but he specifies that the goals Christians pursue are different. We're to focus on the glory of the age to come, not on the worldly pursuits of pleasure, profit, and position. The old saying that Christians shouldn't be so heavenly minded that they're of no earthly good is true as far as it goes, but in today's world Christians' earthly good *depends* on our heavenly mindedness. This reminds me of C. S. Lewis's remark that the Christians who did the most for the present age were those who thought the most of the next.[5]

Making It Understandable

By fully engaging in every area of culture—education, art, politics, business, media, science—we're following Paul's example. "I have become all things to all people, that by all means I might save some" (1 Corinthians 9:22). The principle behind Paul's actions is what Christian thinkers call "contextualization," the idea of translating gospel truth into language understood by our culture. Cross-cultural missionaries and Bible translators have been doing this for centuries. They put the unchanging truth of the gospel into language that fits the changing context and culture they're trying to reach. *Contextualization* simply means translating the gospel—in both word and deed—into understandable terms appropriate to the audience.

Genna, my seven-year-old daughter, loves going to her Sunday school class for various reasons. She loves seeing her friends and singing her favorite songs. But she also loves to learn from her capable and creative teacher. He works hard to use language, concepts, and illustrations that she and the other children in the class will understand as he faithfully teaches them the Bible. And as a result, Genna gets it. She walks away Sunday after Sunday excited about what she's learned. This thrills Kim and me. We're both grateful that her teacher understands the need to contextualize.

Similarly, every English Bible translation is an effort to contextualize the Scriptures (originally written in Hebrew and Greek for ancient peoples) for an English-speaking audience of today.

Contextualization also involves building relationships with people who don't believe. We don't expect them to come to us; we go to them. We meet them where they are. We enter into their world by seeking to identify with their struggles, their likes, their dislikes, their ideas. Chuck Colson speaks of it as entering into people's stories:

> We must enter into the stories of the surrounding culture, which takes real listening.... We connect with the literature, music, theater, arts, and issues that express the existing culture's hopes, dreams, and fears. This builds a bridge by which we can show how the gospel can enter and transform those stories.[6]

Edith Schaeffer, wife of the late Francis Schaeffer, wrote about a visit the two of them made to San Francisco in 1968. One night they went to Fillmore West to hang out with the druggies and hippies and take in a light show. She records how heartbroken they were as they witnessed on that night "the lostness of humanity in search of 'peace' where there is no peace." She concluded, "A time of listening is needed—listening to what the next generation is saying, listening to the words of the music they are listening to, listening to the meaning behind the words. If true communication is to continue, there is a language to be learned."[7]

Contextualization begins with a broken heart for the lost and a driving desire to help them understand God's liberating truth. Only by real listening and learning can we hope to persuasively communicate God's unchanging Word (the Bible) to our constantly changing world.

Sadly, some well-meaning Christians conclude otherwise. For these Christians contextualization means the same thing as compromise. They believe it means giving people what they want and telling people what they want to hear. What they misunderstand, however, is that contextualization means giving people *God's answers* (which they may not want) to the questions they're really asking and in ways they can understand.

This misunderstanding of contextualization has led these people to argue that cultural reflection and contextualization are at best distractions, at worst sinful. They admonish us to abandon these things and focus simply on the Bible. While this sounds virtuous, it ends up being foolish for two reasons. First, as we've already seen, the Bible itself exhorts us to understand our times so that we can reach our changing world with God's eternal truth. To not contextualize, therefore, is a sin. And, second, we all live inescapably within a particular cultural framework that shapes the way we think about everything. So if we don't work hard to understand our context, we'll not only fail in our task to effectively communicate the gospel, but we'll also find it impossible to avoid being negatively shaped by a world we don't understand.

In a recent interview pastor Tim Keller put it this way: "To overcontextualize to a new generation means you can make an idol out of their culture, but to undercontextualize to a new generation means you can make an idol out of the culture you come from. So there's no avoiding it."

Whether translating the Bible or developing relationships with non-Christians, we're to be missionary minded in everything we do. That takes work—the hard effort of maintaining the big picture and communicating comprehensibly and compellingly to those who don't share our convictions and worldview. Therefore, every day and in every circumstance, we need to be consciously and rigorously translating our faith into the language of the culture we're trying to reach.

This is the challenge: If you don't contextualize enough, no one's life will be transformed, because they won't understand you. But (and this is what we'll look at next) if you contextualize too much, no one's life will be transformed, because you won't be challenging their deepest assumptions and calling them to change.

Avoid Being Culturally Relaxed

Becoming "all things to all people" does *not* mean fitting in with the fallen patterns of this world so that there is no distinguishable difference between Christians and non-Christians. While rightly living "in the world," we must avoid the extreme of accommodation—being "of the world." It happens when Christians, in their attempt to make proper contact with the world, go out of their way to adopt worldly styles, standards, and strategies.

When Christians try to eliminate the countercultural, unfashionable features of the biblical message because those features are unpopular in the wider culture—for example, when we reduce sin to a lack of self-esteem, deny the exclusivity of Christ, or downplay the reality of knowable absolute truth—we've moved from contextualization to compromise. When we accommodate our culture by jettisoning key themes of the gospel, such as suffering, humility, persecution, service, and self-sacrifice, we actually do our world more harm than good. For love's sake compromise is to be avoided at all costs.

As we have already seen, the lordship of Christ has a sense of *totality:* Christ's truth covers everything, not just "spiritual" or "religious" things. But it also has a sense of *tension.* As Lord, Jesus not only calls us to himself; he also calls us to break with everything that conflicts with his lordship.

In an article titled "Calling Christian Rebels," journalist Marcia Segelstein describes the cost of being a Christian in our current culture: "It means taking unpopular stands on highly charged issues such as abortion, homosexuality, and divorce. It means risking derision, humiliation, and scorn. It means looking at the way things are and—when they undermine the Word of God—challenging them."[8]

In this sense Christians will often be troublesome to our culture. Devotion to God's authority will bring us into conflict with any authority that challenges his. Loyalty to God's standards will inevitably cause us to clash with the standards of this world.

In seeking to engage and connect, Christians must remember that God hasn't called his people to be popular. He has commanded us to be faithful, even in the face of mockery, criticism, and persecution. The truth is, many in this world will not take kindly to those who follow Jesus, as Jesus himself pointed out (see Matthew 5:11). Since he told us the world would hate us, something's dangerously wrong if we achieve popularity with the world. Contextualization without compromise must be our goal.

The greatest model for this is, of course, the incarnation of Christ. Here God "contextualized" himself by taking on human flesh. Jesus Christ became fully human—one of us. He entered our world, spoke our language, and met us where we are, making deep contact. Jesus completely engaged us. But because he was without sin, his contact resulted in collision. His refusal to fit in eventually led to his execution. He contextualized without compromise right to the bitter end.

As we come into contact with the world, we, too, must always resist its ways. The ideas, values, and passions of the kingdom of God will always collide with the ideas, values, and passions of the kingdom of this world. And where this collision happens, we need to stand our ground.

We could summarize it this way: instead of being culturally removed on the one hand or culturally relaxed on the other, we should seek to be culturally *resistant*. We're making contact with the world while colliding with its ways. We're culturally engaged without being culturally absorbed. We're to maintain a dissonant relationship to the world without isolating ourselves from it.

Mike Metzger of the Clapham Institute outlines the tragic results when we fail to maintain the tension between purity and proximity:

> Being salt and light demands two things: We practice purity
> in the midst of a fallen world and yet we live in proximity to
> this fallen world. If you don't hold up both truths in tension,

you invariably become useless and separated from the world
God loves. For example, if you only practice purity apart
from proximity to the culture, you inevitably become pietis-
tic, separatist, and conceited. If you live in close proximity to
the culture without also living in a holy manner, you become
indistinguishable from fallen culture and useless in God's
kingdom.[9]

We must not fear being different. If we do, we'll never make a
difference. It's only as we faithfully refuse to fit in that we unleash
God's renewing power in this world. So in our attempt to make contact, we must always beware of leaning over so far that we fall in.

We, His Demonstration Community

Meeting people where they are is only the first step in the process of
engagement, not the last. As we deeply engage unbelievers, we're to do
so in ways that reveal the beautiful distinctiveness of a life gripped by
the gospel. We make known just how fundamentally different we are
in how we understand and approach business, finances, work, sexual-
ity, human life—everything!

This is what it means to be "resident aliens." We reside in this
world, but we're not of the world. Our lives exhibit an alternative way
of living, a new way of being human. The goal is to positively demonstrate what God had in mind when he originally designed things.
Renewing the culture God's way can be done only by God's people
diligently living in accordance with God's unfashionable ways. We
transform this world by being God's unfashionable society.

The late Harvie Conn, professor of urban church planting at
Westminster Theological Seminary, used the analogy of a model home
to describe all this. Jesus, the kingdom developer, has begun building
new housing on a tract of earth's land, purchased with his blood. He
has erected a model home as an exhibition of what will eventually fill

the whole world. God intends the church to be that model home. We're his demonstration community. We're to put the rule of Christ on display, showing the unbelieving world what human life and community can look like with God at the center.

This is both our privilege and our responsibility.

Unfashionably United

Our cultural tendency is to surround ourselves with
mirrors rather than windows.

— COLIN DURIEZ

•••••••

AS I SAT WATCHING my daughter's kindergarten musical—watching
her sing and dance and laugh on stage with friends she adores—I was
surprised by a rush of sadness that overcame me.

Some of Genna's friends are white, some Hispanic, some black.
Some come from families having very little, some from wealthy families. Some come from single-parent homes, others from homes where
mom and dad are happily married. Some are physically uncoordi-
nated, while others are already remarkably athletic. But to my six-
year-old daughter and her friends, none of these differences makes a
difference. They love one another and enjoy one another's company.
They don't even seem to notice those things that, in time, will tend to
separate them.

To be sure, Americans have embraced new attitudes on many of
these issues. But powerful social habits remain. By the time Genna
and her friends are in high school, our culture will have tried to convince them to join "their own kind." Over time they'll be informally
segregated into cliques: cheerleaders with cheerleaders, nerds with
nerds, jocks with jocks, artists with artists. The rich will be influenced
to stick with the rich, the poor with the poor, blue collar with blue collar, white collar with white collar.

They'll be told (many by their parents) that smart people hang out with smart people, leaving all the "slower" ones to group with themselves. Movies, magazine covers, and TV shows will influence them to believe that beautiful people should enjoy life with other beautiful people, leaving the unattractive to their own groupings.

By the time they reach adulthood, many of these young friends will be torn apart by the very differences God intends for us to celebrate and enjoy—differences that make each of us unique.

During the musical my daughter's eyes met mine, and she waved and smiled. I did my best to hold back my tears and smile back. Unexpectedly for me, a time intended for sweet memory making had brought a moment of sorrow. I sat there groaning inwardly for my daughter, who would soon be pressured to view human life and community very differently than she does now—very differently, in fact, than God intended.

Relational Loss

What I experienced that afternoon was the sad reality that this world is irrefutably tribal. In spite of how open and freethinking we believe our society has become, segregation is still fashionable—now more than ever, in some ways. We segregate by age and socioeconomic class as well as by race, physical appearance, and cultural background. We're grouped according to likes and dislikes, preferences and personality traits. We form clans of people who all look, talk, think, and act the same.

Some of this separation is both understandable and unavoidable. From elementary school through high school, academic institutions separate students according to age, recognizing the benefit of age-appropriate teaching. But for the most part, when people separate from those who are different, they miss out on so many things intended to enhance human life and relationships.

In *The Four Loves* C. S. Lewis mentions two friends, Ronald and

Charles. After Charles died, Lewis realized there was no consolation to be found in the possibility that he and the surviving friend might now actually "get" more of each other as a result. "Far from having more of Ronald, having him 'to myself' now that Charles is away, I have less of Ronald." He would never again, for example, observe Ronald's unique reaction to one of Charles's jokes. Lewis notes, "In each of my friends there is something that only some other friend can fully bring out. By myself I am not large enough to call the whole man into activity; I want other lights than my own to show all his facets."[1]

The same dynamic of relational loss is at work when we segregate according to kind. We see and experience much less, not more, when we gravitate toward and surround ourselves with those who are just like us. When young are separated from old, rich from poor, black from white, our world becomes a much smaller and less remarkable place. Our preferences and perspectives remain plain and narrow. We lose sight of the beauty and the brilliance that accompany diversity.

To experience the full range of what it means to be fearfully and wonderfully made—to be fully human—we must avoid tribal-mindedness. And Christians ought to be leading the way.

But are we?

Tribal-Minded Versus Mission-Minded

You would expect followers of Christ to be the people who most resist tribal-mindedness. After all, we're the ones who believe all people are made by God in his image and are therefore endowed with dignity and value. We believe the courts of heaven will be occupied by people of all colors, ages, shapes, and sizes, from every tribe, tongue, and nation. So we of all people should be celebrating and learning from the wide range of human differences.

Sadly, though, as we'll see, we Christians tend to be just as tribal as the world around us. And this is a shame, because Christians are called to be unfashionable by being mission-minded, not tribal-minded like everyone else.

There's a radical difference between tribal and missionary mind-sets. The highest value of the tribal-minded is self-protection. Since these people feel safest around those just like them, they ask, "How can I protect myself from those who are different?" They intentionally surround themselves with those who think the way they think, like the things they like, and despise the things they despise.

We all seek out sameness, as John Seel notes: "We cope by settling into our safe intellectual cliques—our favorite blog, cable channel, or e-zine—where our own views are reinforced and applauded. Without really trying we can easily lose sight of the wider horizon and fail to listen to those who do not think as we do."

As a result tribal-minded people live with a sense of superiority, looking down on those who are unlike them. (I can relate. For half my life I was convinced that surfers like me were far cooler than anyone else on the face of this earth.) This is the fashionable posture of our culture.

In contrast, the highest aim of mission-minded people is not self-protection but self-sacrifice. Mission-minded people exist primarily not for themselves but for others. They're willing to set aside personal preferences in service to those with different preferences. They're willing to be inconvenienced, di›mforted, and spent for the well-being of others.

This difference between mission-mindedness and tribal-mindedness is illustrated well in a note I received recently from my good friend Mike about a recent conversation he had with his wife, Nicole:

> Nicole and I were in downtown Fort Lauderdale today. As we were leaving, we passed a park. It was a really nice park, but there was a whole group of homeless people hanging out there. I commented to Nicole that, as nice as the park was, I wouldn't be able to just walk the kids through the park if we lived down there.
>
> Her response to me stung. She said, "Yes you would. You'd just have to go into the park for a different reason. You

could go in and pass out bag lunches." Then she said, "Christians need to remember that, given God's mission, they exist for the city; the city doesn't exist for them."

Ouch!

Nicole understands rightly the gospel's demand for this unfashionable mind-set, because the gospel is the story of God sacrificing himself for others.

The Reach of Reconciliation

Some of my closest friends today are people I would never have hung out with in high school. That's as it should be—the work of God the Son reconciling us to God the Father must also result in our reconciliation with one another.

When we come to God through repentance and faith in Christ, we come into a new relationship with God's people, many of whom are quite different from us. The church exemplifies a radically unusual (and unfashionable) social order because it integrates people who are very unlike one another.

In Paul's day the world was rigidly divided between Jew and Gentile, slave and free, male and female. Those walls of separation were thick, and the groups on each side were hostile. But that didn't stop Paul from boldly proclaiming God's intention to establish a new community—the church—that not only included all these but also allowed them to enjoy deeply interdependent relationships.

As Paul argued for the Gentiles' place in God's redemptive plan, he said, "There is no distinction between Jew and Greek; for the same Lord is Lord of all, abounding in riches for all who call on Him" (Romans 10:12, NASB). As Paul decried certain Jewish leaders for teaching that the sign of circumcision was a condition for justification, he wrote, "There is neither Jew nor Greek, there is neither slave nor free man, there is neither male nor female; for you are all one in

Christ Jesus" (Galatians 3:28, NASB). And when he addressed class distinctions threatening to divide the church, he asserted our newness in Christ, in which "there is no distinction between Greek and Jew, circumcised and uncircumcised, barbarian, Scythian, slave and freeman, but Christ is all, and in all" (Colossians 3:11, NASB).

Paul kept affirming a foundational reality that always accompanies true gospel belief: when God makes us one with Christ, he also makes us one with each other, removing the barriers of separation erected by our society.

In contrast to the tribal-mindedness of the world around us, the church is to bring together people who would remain separated in any other sector of society. The divisive and fundamentally worldly notions of class, race, economics, and age prove to be painful sources of loneliness, fragmentation, and alienation in the modern world—things the church should strive against in establishing a new community.

Segregated Church

Since the gospel is the good news that God reconciles us not only to himself but also to one another, the church should be breaking down barriers, not erecting them. God intends the church to be demonstrating what community looks like when God's reconciling power is at work. Sadly, however, segregation seems to be as fashionable inside the church as outside.

Most churches would agree that any segregation arising from racial or economic bigotry runs contrary to the nature of the gospel and should not be tolerated. But there's another segregation, perhaps more subtle, that many churches today have embraced. Following the lead of the advertising world, many churches and worship services target specific age groups to the exclusion of others. They forget that, according to the Bible, the church is an all-age community, and instead they organize themselves around distinctives dividing the generations: Busters, Boomers, Millennials, Generations X, Y, and Z. Many churches offer a traditional service for the tribe who prefer older music and a contemporary service for the tribe who prefer newer music.

I understand the good intentions behind these seemingly harmless efforts, but they evidence a fundamental failure to comprehend the heart of the gospel. We're not only feeding toxic tribalism; we're also saying the gospel can't successfully bring these two different groups together. It's a declaration of doubt about the unifying power of God's gospel. Generational appeal in worship is an unintentional admission that the gospel is powerless to join together what man has separated.

Building the church on stylistic preferences or age appeal (whether old or young) is just as contrary to the reconciling effect of the gospel as building it on class, race, or gender distinctions. In a recent interview J. I. Packer said, "If worship styles are so fixed that what's being offered fits the expectations, the hopes, *even the prejudices,* of any one of these groups as opposed to the others, I don't believe the worship style glorifies God."

The soul-shrinking by-product of this type of tribalism is that it prevents us from knowing God deeply. The only way to know him deeply is to have many different types of Christian people in your life, since each person will help to reveal a part of God that you can't see by yourself. This means the great tragedy of segregation isn't so much that we see less of each other but that in separating from each other we see less of God. To become a big Christian, you must know a big God. And all of us need other lights than our own to see more of his myriad facets.

One of the leading ways the church can testify to God's unifying power before our segregated world is to establish and maintain congregations that transcend cultural barriers, including age. Todd Pruitt, pastor of Metro East Baptist Church in Wichita, is a good example of this. He recently wrote:

At our church, we have made some deliberate choices not to segregate along lines of age, cultural backgrounds, musical preference, etc. There is little doubt that dividing along these lines "works," in that people often prefer everything to be designed around what makes them most comfortable—their prejudices. But doesn't the gospel lead us toward putting down these impulses? Doesn't the gospel move us out of our comfort zones so that we might take hold of the unity that Christ has already given us?[2]

Maintaining Unity

Not long ago I had the privilege of meeting with Chuck Colson for coffee. He was remarkably gracious, humble, encouraging, hopeful, and intelligent. We talked for more than an hour about life and ministry. We talked about the good, the bad, and the ugly of the evangelical movement. He spoke of his concern over the way we allow our differences (important as they may be) to become divisions. He sadly admitted that in his experience the Christian community can be just as cold as the political community. At one point he said, "I've seen more backbiting inside the church than I can remember seeing in the halls of political power working as President Nixon's hatchet man." Stunning—and sad!

Our conversation turned to how destructive it can be when Christians downplay or altogether ignore Ephesians 4:1–7, where Paul makes it clear that unity is something we as followers of Christ already possess—not something we must achieve, but something we must maintain. Our goal is to preserve and uphold what we already have. The implication is that if we don't strive to maintain our unity in the Spirit, we'll become divided.

> I therefore, a prisoner for the Lord, urge you to walk in a
> manner worthy of the calling to which you have been called,
> with all humility and gentleness, with patience, bearing with
> one another in love, eager to maintain the unity of the Spirit

in the bond of peace. There is one body and one Spirit—just
as you were called to the one hope that belongs to your call—
one Lord, one faith, one baptism, one God and Father of all,
who is over all and through all and in all. But grace was
given to each one of us according to the measure of Christ's
gift.

Our unity in the Spirit exists by virtue of the fact that each Christian is individually united to Christ by the Spirit and is therefore linked with all other Christians. When God the Father made us one with God the Son through God the Spirit, we became one with each other. Just as bicycle spokes are linked by their common attachment to the hub, so Christians are linked by their common attachment to Christ. In him, Christians of every tribe, tongue, and nation become brothers and sisters. Though we're all distinct, all different, in Christ we're no longer divided. We don't always act unified, but that doesn't change the fact that in Christ we are one.

This means that ultimately there should be no irreconcilable differences among us, since our common identity in Christ transcends our differences. There will be distinctives and differences among Christians, but there should never be divisions between true followers of Christ. Differences are good; divisions are bad. We are one family, united to one Christ, by one Spirit.

As a believer in Jesus, you're specifically mentioned by him in John 17:20–21, where he prays, "I do not ask for these only [the apostles], but also for those who will believe in me through their word, *that they may all be one,* just as you, Father, are in me, and I in you, that they also may be in us, so that the world may believe that you have sent me."

It's amazing to know that Jesus interceded for us and still does intercede for us. It's also amazing to see *what* he prays for us: Jesus wants us to be unified—to be one as he and the Father are one. I don't fully understand what that means, but I do know I want it to be a reality.

When It's Hard

Recognizing and maintaining our unity can be hard for me, particularly when I encounter a brother or sister in Christ who has theological and biblical convictions that differ from mine. My theological convictions run deep, and I care passionately about truth. I recognize the absolute necessity of "rightly handling the word of truth" (2 Timothy 2:15). So I still struggle with this.

And when it comes to our sincere doctrinal differences, I've come to realize there aren't easy answers. How do Calvinist Christians maintain unity with Arminian Christians? How do Baptist Christians maintain unity with Presbyterian Christians? How do dispensational Christians maintain unity with covenantal Christians? How do we properly understand and apply the age-old saying (usually credited to Augustine): "In essentials, unity; in nonessentials, liberty; in all things, charity"?

I have to keep thinking hard and working hard at these things. But a couple of truths are clear to me.

Gospel on Display

First, God intends his people to be a visual model of the gospel. He wants us to live our lives together in such a way that we demonstrate the good news of reconciliation before the watching world.

When new members join New City Church, they promise "to promote the unity, purity, and peace of the church." One of the quickest ways to break this vow is to gossip—to "chatter idly about others." This seemingly innocent activity can cause a world of hurt. The corrective is found in the ninth commandment, as the Heidelberg Catechism explains:

> God's will is that I never give false testimony against anyone, twist no one's words, not gossip or slander, nor join in condemning anyone without a hearing or without a just cause.

Rather, in court and everywhere else, I should avoid lying and deceit of every kind; these are devices the devil himself uses, and they would call down on me God's intense anger. I should love the truth, speak it candidly, and openly acknowledge it. And I should do what I can to guard and advance my neighbor's good name.[3]

I'm convinced that most divisions in the church would never happen if we kept this one commandment. When we sin against our brother or sister, what we fail to realize is that, in Christ, we are united. A sin (such as slander) against any one of us is a sin against all of us. When we sin against a brother or sister, we sin against ourselves. It's like shooting ourselves in the foot, only much worse.

We need to maintain the unity we have in Christ by ridding ourselves of "all hatred and prejudice, and whatever else may hinder us from godly union and concord."[4] Lacking love for the body (and for any individuals in the body) shows a lack of love for the Head of the body. If we love Christ, we will love one another. This is what inspired these lines of John Newton:

May we abide in union with each other and the Lord,
and possess in sweet communion joys which earth cannot
afford.

In Chuck Colson's book *The Faith*, he writes, "Reconciliation within the church requires a surrender of pride and a willingness to put God's interests over our own interests. Peacemaking within the congregation should be a high priority."

Francis Schaeffer once noted that bitter divisions among Christians give the world the justification they're looking for to disbelieve the gospel. But when reconciliation, peacemaking, and unity are on display inside the church, that becomes a powerful witness to this fractured world. "Just as I have loved you," Jesus commanded, "you also are to love one another. *By this all people will know that you are my disciples,* if you have love for one another" (John 13:34–35).

Facing External Threat

A second truth about this that's clear to me can be illustrated in ancient history, as written about recently by my friend Reggie Kidd:

Following the deaths of the Spartan King Leonidas and "his brave three hundred" at Thermopylae in 480 B.C., the various Greek city-states decided they needed to pull together. Xerxes' gargantuan army and navy were poised to overwhelm Greece, indeed the whole of Europe. At the eleventh hour the Greeks realized they needed each other.

Traditionally, Greece looked to Sparta for leadership on land and to Athens for leadership on the sea. But in this case there were misgivings about giving Athens command of the city-states' combined fleets (despite Athens' contributing the largest number of ships). Herodotus isn't clear whether the reluctance was due to lack of confidence in or envy against Athens, or due simply to a recognition of Sparta's moral capital.

The point is: Athens "got it," to quip Herodotus: civil war in the face of an external threat is suicide.... When the enemy is at the gate, that's not the time to be throwing each other out the window.

Rather than lobby for their traditional right to command, Athens accepted Spartan command of the navy as well as of the army. The result: two brilliant victories—one by Greece's combined navies (at Salamis) and one by Greece's combined armies (at Plataea)—and one huge and final retreat by Xerxes....

There are times that call for a sense of measure and proportion—times when you need not to be doing a smack

down on each other. Fifth century B.C. Greece figured it
out. Will we?[5]

The truth is, we need one another—we need to be united. And
the only way to maintain our unity in Christ is by showing our commitment to him through our commitment to one another.

The world desperately needs to see this. The power of our witness
is in large part due to the compelling, nonsegregated society we
demonstrate to the world around us.

One could say that the survival of evangelical Christianity in the
twenty-first century will depend in large measure on how serious we
are about believing and applying Ephesians 4:1–7. The battle is fierce;
the enemies are ruthless. We need each other now more than ever!

Making the Difference
Together

The fellowship of the church is part of God's good
news to men. It imparts to the gospel one of its most
thrilling notes—that when Christ saves a man he not
only saves him from his sin, he saves him from his
solitude.

— FRANK COLQUHOUN

IN THAT GREAT BIBLE PASSAGE known as his high priestly prayer, Jesus
talks with his Father about his disciples: "I do not ask that you take
them out of the world, but that you keep them from the evil one. *They
are not of the world, just as I am not of the world*" (John 17:15–16).

Jesus goes on in this prayer to indicate that he's making his
requests, not just for that band of men who were with him at the time,
but also for *us*—for all who would believe in Christ through the gospel
message taken into the world by these apostles. Jesus prays for *our*
unity and for *our* impact: "that they may all be one, just as you, Father,
are in me, and I in you, that they also may be in us, *so that the world
may believe* that you have sent me" (17:21).

I have every reason to believe that Jesus prays this same prayer
before the throne of God for you and for me every day, unceasingly.
He prays that we, the people of God, would be in the world but not
of the world—against the world for the world—and that we would be

God's alternative society, making daily contact with the world and making a difference, like salt and light.

And his intention is that we make this difference *together.* He doesn't want any of us to be worried about standing alone in our unfashionableness. We're called to do this as a team and as a team of teams. In fact, that's the only way our mission can ever be accomplished.

New for a Reason

To get the right perspective on this togetherness, let's review what's really new about us.

As I mentioned earlier, Christians aren't perfect people, but we are fundamentally *different* people. If you're a Christian, you've been radically transformed from the inside out. Your disposition, your desires, and the entire direction of your life have been essentially altered. You may not yet be *completely* changed, but you're already *fundamentally* changed. You've been lifted to new heights.

As C. S. Lewis says in *Mere Christianity,* "God became man to turn creatures into sons: not simply to produce better men of the old kind but to produce a new kind of man. It is not like teaching a horse to jump better and better but like turning a horse into a winged creature."[1]

This newness means you're no longer sin-centered at your core. The Bible tells us that Christians are new creatures with new natures. The old things have passed away, and all things have become new (see 2 Corinthians 5:17).

All this newness is for a reason. In a variety of ways, the New Testament makes this point repeatedly: once you did not know God, and your life showed it, but now you do know God, *so you must live godly lives.* "Put off your old self," Paul tells us, "which belongs to your former manner of life and is corrupt through deceitful desires." Instead of our living in that old way, he tells us "to be renewed in the spirit of your minds, and to put on the new self, created after the likeness of

God in true righteousness and holiness" (Ephesians 4:22–24). In essence, he's telling Christians to become *practically* what they already are *positionally.* We're to live in a way that's consistent with who God saved us and remade us to be. New people must live new lives.

It makes no sense, Paul wants us to know, to keep living according to the old ways. Christians are to be marked, perhaps first and foremost, by a trend of always putting off old ways and putting on new ways. We must *become* what we *are.*

But this is more than just living differently as individuals. For the church, putting off the old and putting on the new is also our responsibility as a new community so that we make a difference *together.*

Individualism

Recently I was happy to be invited to a gathering of local pastors to discuss foster care in our community and ways in which our churches can be more effectively involved in helping children who need such care. Sitting there, I realized that many of us had never been in the same room with one another for the purpose of discussing a social need that the church is capable of meeting. This was the first time we had stepped out of our own little worlds and *together* entered into the one world we're all called to reach and change. We joined heads, hearts, and hands, realizing for the first time that "a cord of three strands is not quickly broken" (Ecclesiastes 4:12, NIV).

I've never met a pastor from our area who doesn't genuinely want to make a difference in this community. They all want to see God-centered change. The same is true, I believe, about most Christians. We truly want to have an impact in our community, but too often we don't achieve anything significant because we want to do everything ourselves. We're so caught up with our individual goals, agendas, and projects that we forget how desperately we need each other. Our impact is weakened because, like the world around us, Christians have succumbed to individualism.

Individuality—as opposed to individualism—is a good thing. Each of us is "fearfully and wonderfully made" (Psalm 139:14), uniquely fashioned by our Creator so that no two of us are exactly the same. *Individualism,* however, is bad. It is a fundamentally worldly way of understanding what it means to be human. Stamped into the fabric of our modern society is the idea that the individual is the primary center of reality, the ultimate standard of value. We live in a culture where there are no longer any obligations to others. The locus of all authority is squarely fixed on the individual self. This approach devalues the role of the many in favor of the one. Togetherness and community are radically diminished. It's all about "me," not "we."

In the Bible, however, we discover that while we're called by God as individuals, we're called *into* his new community, the church.

In our day the word *church* tends to make us think of buildings and institutions; we assume it refers exclusively to a particular structure or establishment. In the Bible, however, the word for *church* literally means "the called-out ones"—those individuals who have been called out of darkness and called together into the light, thus forming God's new community (what the early church fathers called the *communio sanctorum,* or the communion of saints). Therefore the church is first about community, not construction; about people, not programs.

This means there's no such thing as Christian individualism; it's an oxymoron. The church is meant to be a God-formed community of people who have abandoned the notion that life can and should be lived in isolation. Christians are *connected* people—connected with each other by God the Father, through God the Son, in God the Spirit.

This is why we make a difference in our community by *being a different community*—Christians working with other Christians, churches with other churches. When we exhibit corporate togetherness, we show the world God's original intention and design, not only for individual human lives, but also for human communities.

Again, it's like that model-home concept I mentioned earlier, which I learned from Harvie Conn. We're God's demonstration community of the rule of Christ, and by living the new life in the new community according to God's new standards, we show a hurting, desperate world what human life and human community were originally intended to be—and what they'll one day look like perfectly. We give them a sampling of heaven on earth.

God Critiques by Creating

One of my goals as a senior pastor is for our pastoral staff to embody gospel-centered community so we serve as a model to the rest of our church. How do we seek to do this? We laugh with one another, cry with one another, love one another, serve one another, exhort one another, and forbear with one another. We pray together, read the Bible together, and serve together. We share in one another's pleasures and pains. And we try, by God's grace, to "stir up one another to love and good works" (Hebrews 10:24). We work hard at becoming the kind of community we want our church to become.

Not surprisingly, our commitment to demonstrate God-centered community has spread throughout our church, and our church has increasingly become what we long for our surrounding area to become. As this continues to happen, our church models what human life and community can look like when fueled by the gospel.

That's the way God does things—he critiques by creating. He shows us what's wrong by giving us a model of what's right. Think about the incarnation of Jesus: God the Son becoming man, taking on human flesh, and showing us perfect humanity. God critiqued what was wrong with sinful humanity by showing us, in Christ, what humanity was originally intended to be and what redeemed humanity will one day be again.

The church joins with Christ in showing the world what's wrong with it. Christ, the Head of the church, did it by demonstrating what humanity is intended to be; the church, as Christ's body, does it by demonstrating what human community is intended to be.

We work at becoming together what God wants the rest of the world to become. The purpose of God's people is to show a watching world what will one day fill the whole earth.

If Christians care to make a difference in this world, it has less to do with gaining political power or electing the right officials and far more to do with actually living out our new life together in this new community—the church—before the watching world. Our best approach for reaching people in today's world is not by going door to door and giving evangelistic presentations, passing out evangelistic tracts, or blanketing our cities with evangelistic crusades. Our best approach is living with the people we're trying to reach and showing them what human life and community look like when the gospel is believed and embraced.

God's great evangelistic tool is the church—this new, counter-cultural community in which the fellowship of the Father, Son, and Holy Spirit comes to expression in the unity, community, and joy of God's people. As we live together in a way that's consistent with who we've been remade to be, we become a blessing to the world by showing it how sweet life can be in a community of individuals who love one another, care for one another, defer to one another, are patient with one another, and serve one another. The world will take notice of a community of men and women who refreshingly and joyfully bear one another's burdens and who actively look to lay down their lives for others in need because Jesus laid down his life for them. When the world sees that Christians want to help people because God has helped them, they'll begin to ask what makes us so different. A faithful presentation of the gospel to our world, in other words, requires Christian community on full display.

The church must always remember that she *is* God's mission to the world, making a difference by being different. In the next several chapters, we'll explore specific guidelines in the New Testament for what that difference really looks like.

Part 3

The Community

A Truthful Community

During times of universal deceit, telling the truth becomes a revolutionary act.

— GEORGE ORWELL

EPHESIANS MAY WELL BE the preeminent New Testament book on the church. The first half of this letter from the apostle Paul looks at the church *positionally*, while the second half focuses on the church *practically*—the way we live in this dark world as the body of Christ, his transformed, light-bearing community.

In the heart of the practical conclusion to the book, we find a series of verses that are well worth a closer look as we think about our corporate calling to make a difference by being different. This passage begins with an exhortation quoted in the previous chapter, where Paul urges us "to put off your old self, which belongs to your former manner of life and is corrupt through deceitful desires, and to be renewed in the spirit of your minds, and to put on the new self, created after the likeness of God in true righteousness and holiness" (4:22–24). Paul then goes on to outline six concrete ways in which this putting-off, putting-on dynamic needs to take place within the Christian community.

In most commentaries this passage is explained and applied to individuals without much regard for the corporate, churchwide dimension. But Paul here is going beyond exhorting us about our individual responsibility to put off old ways and put on new ways; he's exhorting us as a community to do these things *together*.

These verses are missionary verses. Paul is telling us as a corporate entity, as the people of God, what kind of community we need to be in order to carry out God's mission. He lays out six defining marks that ought to identify the community of God—things that should mark individual local churches as we bring the reality of the next world into this world.

The first of these defining marks is truthfulness. What I want to show in this chapter is how compelling our influence for God's kingdom becomes when we carefully and insightfully choose truth over falsehood.

Putting Off Lies, Putting On Truth

Paul writes, "Having put away falsehood, let each one of you speak the truth with his neighbor, for we are members one of another" (Ephesians 4:25). We should be a *truthful* community. That's the first of the six concrete guidelines Paul gives us here for God's demonstration community. We're to put off lies and fully embrace truth.

Why is this such a critical step in our witness to the world? Because we live in a trustless culture, and people are hungry for an alternative to that trustlessness.

Few people trust anyone these days, and it's for a good reason: too few people these days are trustworthy. Lies, betrayal, hypocrisy—these things mark every institution and every relationship to some degree. Everyone seems to be a spin doctor. It's really hard to know who's being real and who's not. We wonder, *Is she telling the truth? Is he trying to rip me off? Who might stab me in the back? Does he really love me? Is my wife cheating on me?*

Since all of us face questions every day about whom we can trust, we find ourselves becoming skeptical of just about everybody—from car salesmen to politicians, from our spouses to our colleagues. We don't trust mechanics, preachers, or lawyers. We live in a perpetual state of suspicion, wondering whom we can really rely on. Who will tell us the truth? Who will be transparent? Who will be honest? We encounter people all the time who are none of these things.

In his book *Trust: The Social Virtues and the Creation of Prosperity,* Francis Fukuyama points out that every culture that has been able to advance its economy, achieve technical proficiency, and develop innovative organizations has been a culture where trust is entrenched in the society. Fukuyama argues compellingly that in comparison with low-trust societies that need to negotiate and often litigate rules and regulations, high-trust societies are able to minimize the cost of doing business and, as a result, advance culture to a high level. Why is this?

Because every healthy, functioning community is built on trust—in your home, in your neighborhood, at work, or wherever relationships among people are critical. Cities, towns, villages, countries, and cultures are all dependent on trust to function properly. Take away trust and you take away community. That's because healthy community relies on people who invest in one another, serve one another, provide for one another, and defer to one another. Without this "one-anotherness" genuine community cannot exist.

But here's the problem: in a culture where people don't trust each other, everyone looks out for himself, not for others. People who don't trust those around them live lives of self-protection *from* others rather than of self-sacrifice *for* others. And this posture ruins the possibility of real community, which in turn hinders the advance of culture.

So we need to somehow regain trust. And to do it, we must regain truth, since trust is built on truth. You can't have community without trust, and you can't have trust without truth. To trust someone, you need to believe he is being honest with you.

The reason it's so hard in our culture to find trustworthy and reliable people is that we've departed from the foundational belief that truth can be known. In the twenty-first century truth is regarded as either unattainable or unnecessary.

In fact, many in our world (including many professing Christians!) have concluded that universal truth doesn't exist at all. They say each person creates truth for himself. They're like the baseball umpire who said, "Let's be honest: there are balls and there are strikes, but they ain't nothin' till I call 'em." According to this view, truth doesn't exist outside of *me;* truth is whatever I say it is, whatever I want it to be.

But when truth is whatever each individual wants it to be, there's no common ground on which trust can be established. So trust disappears. And where trust disappears, genuine, healthy community will disappear. This is why marriages fall apart, homes fall apart, neighborhoods fall apart, countries fall apart, and even churches fall apart—they become distanced from truth. Trust is required for true community, but trust must be built on truth. (It's ironic to me that many of the leaders in the "emergent church" who are championing the recovery of "church as community" are the same ones who are jettisoning the notion of absolute truth—the very foundation on which community can alone be established.)

Trust will disappear in a culture that does away with truth. Our contemporary culture's unwavering commitment to the relativity of truth destroys the foundation for enjoying true, life-giving community.

Service, Not Sabotage

This is where the church, the people of God, must demonstrate what community is intended to be. We're a community founded on truth and formed by truth. We have everything we need from God to be honest, reliable, and dependable—people whose word can be counted on. Our belief in truth and love of truth enables us to be the trustworthy people whom God has called us to be and whom the world needs us to be.

That's what this community called the church is supposed to embody. That's the kind of people God has remade us to be. When we're anything less, the world views us just as suspiciously as it views everyone else and can only wonder about us, *What do they really want from me?*

When the world concludes that we'll say and do anything, true or not, to gain cultural power, they tune us out—and rightfully so. Here's an example: Some Christian writers, in their eagerness to promote America's "Christian" roots and justify Christianity's "rightful claim" to this country, have embraced the Founding Fathers' references to God without acknowledging that the god of Thomas Jefferson, James Madison, and John Adams is one that most orthodox Christians of any tradition wouldn't affirm. "American Christians, who are concerned with truth," writes Preston Jones, "should want to avoid coming to wrong conclusions about history, even when that means giving up cherished ideas about the stuff of their nation's past."[1]

When Christians spin history in a less-than-factual direction, thinking that the end justifies the means, it shows that we're no more trustworthy than anyone else. But when we're trustworthy and factual and real—showing the world that we want to serve them, not sabotage them—the church becomes an incredible breath of fresh air; we make a difference because we're radically different.

"If you seek power before service," Tim Keller says, "you'll neither get power nor serve. If you seek to serve people more than to gain power, you will not only serve people, but you will gain influence." Do you want to have an impact on the world around you? Then serve people in a no-strings-attached manner. When we serve others, and they know we're there to serve them for their good, with no hidden agenda, they tune in to what we say because they see us as trustworthy.

In his book *Respectable Sins,* Jerry Bridges tells about meeting a car salesman years ago who told him, "After I became a Christian, I stopped trying to sell cars and started helping people buy cars." Bridges comments, "His focus changed from how much money he would make to how he could serve people by helping them buy the car that would best fit their needs and their financial situation."[2] Tell me, wouldn't you find that approach to car sales refreshing and appealing? Wouldn't you feel that a salesman like that had earned your repeat business?

And as an aside here, let me ask, is your own focus (and that of your church) more on "selling" God or on helping people find him? Practically speaking, what's the difference? I'd suggest that the difference will be manifested most clearly in genuinely serving others and the straightforward, honest endeavor to meet their true and deepest needs, as only Christ can do through his people.

Being trustworthy is what Paul is talking about when he says the church is to be a community that embodies truth, the one community where what you see is genuinely what you get—no spin, no masks. We're to say what we mean and mean what we say. We let our yes be yes and our no be no.

In this world where everyone's a spin doctor, truthfulness is one fundamental way the church demonstrates what God originally intended community to be.

And there are more. Let's tackle another of the defining marks that Paul gives us in Ephesians.

An Angry Community

Anyone can become angry—that is easy. But to be
angry with the right person, to the right degree, at
the right time, for the right purpose and in the right
way—that is not easy.

— ARISTOTLE

● ● ● ● ● ●

THE CHURCH IS TO BE not only a truthful community but also an
angry community.

Obviously this point needs some explaining!

Here's what Paul says: "Be angry and do not sin; do not let the sun
go down on your anger, and give no opportunity to the devil" (Ephesians 4:26–27). He's not merely allowing us to be angry; he's com-
manding us: "Be angry."

Of course he immediately qualifies this by adding "and do not
sin." But that little "be angry" phrase still seems shocking. What could
it possibly mean?

Anger can be God-centered or self-centered. God-centered anger
is when you get angry because God has been dishonored and his ways
have been maligned. Self-centered anger is when you're angry because
you have been dishonored or *your* ways have been maligned.

We all experience anger, because anger results from hurt, and
there's no way we can go through life without getting hurt. What I
want to show in this chapter is how choosing God-centered anger over
self-centered anger will intensify our influence for God's kingdom in
this world.

Unfashionable Anger

The anger that marks our fallen world is self-centered, not God-centered. It's culturally excusable and even fashionable in our world for people to get angry because their purposes have been thwarted, their desires squelched, their preferences ignored. It's stylish for people to get mad because they've been disrespected, discomforted, or inconvenienced.

But the church is to exhibit an unfashionable type of anger—God-centered anger.

Anger itself isn't always wrong, the Bible tells us. When Jesus walked into the temple and saw that it had been turned into a marketplace, he got angry, overturned the tables, and rebuked the crowd (see John 2:13–17). It was right for him to get angry because God was being dishonored; his ways were being maligned.

When Paul tells us to be angry, he's obviously thinking of the God-centered sort, not the self-centered sort. He's not giving us the right to get angry because we're personally frustrated. He's not talking about being meanspirited, joyless, and out of control. He's not giving us license to lose our temper because somebody annoys us or to hold a grudge because we're irritated. What he's telling us is to be people who *hate the things God hates for the reasons God hates them.*

Hating What God Hates

In his commentary on this verse in Ephesians, John Stott says, "There is great need in the contemporary world for more Christian anger. We human beings compromise with sin in a way in which God never does.… If God hates sin, his people should hate it too."[1]

Our world needs more God-centered anger (and less self-centered anger). Sin and evil and immorality—all these things *should* arouse our anger. The world *needs* to see our anger at evils such as racial violence, torture, genocide, child abuse, drug and sex trafficking, divorce, low educational standards, corporate greed, adultery, and pornography. Sadly, the church is often guilty of ignoring these evils, failing to express God-centered anger at the way God's image bearers—human beings—are being dehumanized, mistreated, and denigrated by one another. We thereby inadvertently communicate to the watching world that God has no social conscience and doesn't care about injustice.

But God is a God of justification *and* justice. He cares deeply, not only about the salvation of individuals, but also about his people being ready and willing to "seek justice, rescue the oppressed, defend the orphan, plead for the widow" (Isaiah 1:17, NRSV). God is angry when justice is not sought, when the oppressed are not rescued, when the orphan is not defended, and when the widow is not pleaded for. When we see how sin causes human beings to treat each other in undignified, unjust ways, we should be incensed, not indifferent! Since God is angry at sin's devastation, God's people should be too.

Why do these things make God angry?

Look with me at another occasion when Jesus was angry, in Mark 3:1–5. One day Jesus "entered the synagogue, and a man was there with a withered hand." Meanwhile the Pharisees in the crowd "watched Jesus, to see whether he would heal him on the Sabbath, so that they might accuse him." Jesus didn't hold back: "He said to the man with the withered hand, 'Come here.' And he said to them, 'Is it lawful on the Sabbath to do good or to do harm, to save life or to kill?' But they were silent."

Notice carefully what comes next: "And he looked around at them *with anger, grieved at their hardness of heart,* and said to the man, 'Stretch out your hand.' He stretched it out, and his hand was restored."

Jesus, the God-man, was *angry.* And then we immediately read that he was also *grieved,* seeing the hardness of the Pharisees' hearts.

God's anger is a grieving anger. It grieves because it sees the devastation that sin has on human life. Jesus was angry because God's ways were being maligned and God was being dishonored by these legalistic

Pharisees. But his anger was fueled by grief—he saw sin's deadening effects in the lives of these hardened Pharisees. It was as if he asked them, "Why do you continue like this? Don't you see that you were created and designed for so much more than this?" It grieved him to see that these Pharisees, because of their sin, were only shadows of what God originally intended for them to be. They had been made to live for so much more.

In *The Great Divorce,* C. S. Lewis describes allegorically the difference between people who are running toward God on their way to heaven and those running away from God on their way to hell. The people moving farther from God become more and more see-through, less solid; they begin losing their substance and coloring. But the people moving closer to God become more and more concrete and brightly colored.

God is grievingly angry when our sin causes us to become less and less of what God created us to be, because we were fearfully and wonderfully made to live for so much more.

Our Grief

Our anger should be a grieving anger as well. When we see immorality and injustice, our anger should be stoked because of the devastating effects these things have on human life and community.

When any of our three children disobey and require punishment—when they show disrespect, don't tell the truth, or whatever the violation might be—my wife and I get angry, and rightfully so. In those moments of disobedience, my children are dishonoring God, refusing to trust him, refusing to obey him. In those moments they're running from God. But our anger toward them is a grieving anger, because we know they were created and designed for something so much better and more satisfying than soul-shrinking sin and disobedience. We grieve because their sin hurts them; it creates distance between them and God by hardening their hearts and searing their consciences. Our anger is stirred up because our love for them is radical—we want to see them become all God designed them to be, not less!

This godly, grieving anger is far different from the kind of anger commonly associated with Christians. Lots of people think of Christians as embittered, angry people, especially in relation to highly charged social issues such as abortion and homosexuality. They view Christians as being frustrated by our culture because things just aren't going our way; our conservative political agenda is being thwarted.

Years ago I was one of five thousand people listening to a panel discussion at a Christian conference. An editor of a conservative political-theological magazine was expressing his frustration with many of the political left-wingers and doing so in an unnecessarily sarcastic and condescending way. When he finished, John Piper (another speaker on the panel) turned to him, and with utmost seriousness and precision, he said, "For a long time I have appreciated your ministry. You are an astute observer of our culture. I read your magazine every month. It's always insightful. But there's one thing missing from your ministry."

The editor looked at Dr. Piper and asked what it was.

"Tears," Piper replied.

The world so often senses our anger, but do they ever sense our grief? They think we're angry simply because we're not getting our way, but I'm afraid they don't feel our sorrow over sin's negative, dehumanizing effects. We fail to communicate our anger in a way that says, "You were made for so much more than this." They assume our anger is only because we're not getting what we want. No wonder they tune us out.

When we see the restlessness and wreckage in people's lives because they're not in relationship with God and they're living sin-filled lives, it should stoke our anger—an anger that arises because we love them and we grieve to see them living for something so destructive when God created them to live for something beautiful and satisfying.

Self-centered anger is not a grieving, love-fueled anger; that's what

God-centered anger is. So does your anger rage because your love for God and your love for others is radical? When people see us hating what God hates because our love for God and people is real and deep, then and only then will they pay attention to our message.

Look Here First

I need to take this one step further and emphasize that God-centered anger is no respecter of persons. It hates sin wherever sin is found—first and foremost in ourselves.

Thomas Fuller, an old Puritan, said: "Be soonest angry with thyself." Self-centered anger points the finger outward first, but God-centered anger points it inward. Self-centered anger is proud; God-centered anger is humble. Self-centered anger first cries out, "Who are you?" God-centered anger first cries out, "Who am I?" Until you first feel the grief and the anger over your own imperfections, you dare not show your grief and anger over the imperfections of others.

Our anger should always be just as fierce over our own sin as over anyone else's. If other people's sin angers you more than your own, you can be sure you're guilty of self-centered anger.

Can you imagine the impression the church and Christians would give to people if we embodied God-centered anger in this way? Instead of weary, passive accommodation and acceptance of our shortcomings, there would be an active engagement with the love and power of Christ to discover and apply his healing and correction across the spectrum of our lives.

Not the least area where our anger ought to be ignited and dealt with is the one we'll focus on next, one that exposes an especially oppressive deception that's rampant in our world today.

Putting Off Stealing

All the blessings we enjoy are divine deposits, committed to our trust on this condition, that they should be dispensed for the benefit of our neighbors.

—JOHN CALVIN

●●●●●●

A THIRD IDENTIFYING MARK Paul lays out for the body of Christ is that we're to be a community that puts off stealing and puts on generosity. "Let the thief no longer steal," Paul writes, "but rather let him labor, doing honest work with his own hands, so that he may have something to share with anyone in need" (Ephesians 4:28).

This world you and I live in is marked by a radical commitment to thievery. I'm not talking about the obvious forms of stealing, such as cheating on taxes or lifting wallets at the fair. I'm talking about a type of robbery happening all around us that most of us never notice.

Every single day attempts are made to steal our time, our talents, and our money, and because it's so out in the open and such a normal part of living in the modern world, we don't even bat an eye.

Let me explain.

The Stealing Strategy

Think about this: the advertising industry spends untold billions of dollars each year trying to steal your time by making you believe that recreation, not work, is the ultimate source of personal fulfillment.

Maybe you've seen the bumper sticker that reads, "I say we fish six days and work one." I'm not a fisherman, so I'd probably be more sympathetic to the one that reads, "I say we surf six days and work one."

That's the approach to life we're encouraged to embrace. We're told to pursue personal comfort and respite regardless of the cost. The good life is a life free of responsibilities. We're told in a thousand different ways that we all deserve a break today—a long one—and that our time is best spent if it's idle. Sit back, relax, enjoy the ride, and take as many vacations as you possibly can, because that's the real goal of human life—not working, not investing yourself in others (or for the good of society as a whole), not making the most of every opportunity, as the Bible teaches us.

To be sure, workaholism is a real danger in our day. But even that is often fueled by the promise that if we work hard enough, we can make enough money to retire early and spend the rest of our days enjoying the real reward—time off.

Think, too, of the amount of advertising money spent every day trying to convince you to expend all your talents and money on yourself here and now instead of investing long term *in* others, *for* others. Life is lived for the moment, we're told. Today is really all that matters, so don't think about the consequences of your decisions or how they'll affect tomorrow.

Advertisers are relentless in their attempts to steal your money by giving you the line that you can't be happy without their product, that the fulfillment you're looking for can always be experienced by buying more of their stuff.

According to recent statistics from the Federal Reserve, "consumer debt in 2008 now stands at $2.6 trillion. The average household in 2008 carried nearly $8,700 in credit card debt."[1] This reveals the dangerous impact of the I-want-it-and-I-want-it-now mentality that advertisers encourage us to embrace. It's especially on display in the lives of twenty-somethings who leave college expecting to immediately enter life with the same status and possessions their parents enjoy.

There's no intention of saving for anything. Even starting out, they deserve a new car and a nice house with new furniture, and a credit card is the expeditious way of getting that lifestyle under way.

But God has equipped you to make a deep, long-term contribution to society in various ways. He's given you different gifts to be exercised, not only within the community of God, but also in service to the world. The world strongly influences us in a thousand ways to take a short view of life—eat, drink, and be merry now because tomorrow may never come. Christians, on the other hand, are to take a longer, more clearheaded view of life, living intentionally and responsibly in order to make contributions to society that will last long after our individual lives in this world are over.

Reason for Generosity

Living in a world where attempts are made every day to steal our time, talents, and money makes people feel cheap and used. They become objects to be marketed to, not persons to be loved and invested in. Every human being is viewed simply as a potential buyer, a market for someone's products. Eventually this dehumanizes us, pushing us to play the same game. We adopt the same Machiavellian mentality, preying on others in the same way we are used ourselves.

Our value, we're told, is based solely on what we're able to buy or sell, which means both buyers and sellers are robbed of something even more precious than time, talents, and money. We're robbed of the dignity that comes from knowing what it means to be a human being fearfully and wonderfully made in the image of God.

The bottom line is that the world's ethic is marked by taking, not giving. But the church can step in here and become an alternative society. We can be a lifesaver for a culture drowning in thievery if we'll only embrace Paul's instruction to distinguish ourselves by being a community not of takers but of givers, always having "something to share with anyone in need" (Ephesians 4:28).

Consider, for instance, the fashionable (and almost automatic) response in our world to getting a pay raise: You elevate your standard of living. You get a nicer car, a bigger house, a home-entertainment center, more expensive clothing. But in the Bible we find the principle that to whom much is given, much is also required (see Luke 12:48). This means, in part, that more income should lead first to increased *giving,* not increased living. Choosing to view something like a financial raise in this way is radically unfashionable—and to the watching world, radically refreshing.

My friend Trevin recently wrote that Christians "can show that money is not lord by demonstrating to the world that all money comes from God, by embracing a mind-set that focuses on eternal investments over temporal benefits, and by showing the world that people matter more than possessions. The best way to subvert the idol of Mammon is by giving it away freely."

Christians ought to be known as the most generous people on the face of this earth—the most generous with our time, our talents, and our money. Why? Because more than anyone else, Christians are to understand that we're owners of nothing and stewards of everything. Everything we have is a gift from God that we're to handle responsibly. The only thing you and I own—the only thing that's really ours—is our sin. Everything else is a blessing from our Creator. Our resources, our time, and our abilities are all gifts from God.

The fact is, we should consider ourselves stewards of everything in our lives—every dollar we earn, every good idea that enters our minds, every position we attain, every privilege we enjoy. We are to steward well all our skills, resources, experiences, influence, and social capital, investing them back into the created order for the good of other people. We're to leverage our God-given resources for the common good, making this society a better place to live for everyone, not just ourselves. As Christians, we'll be held accountable for the way we invest every asset God has given us (see Matthew 25:14–30).

More than anyone else, Christians ought to operate according to the words of the martyred missionary Jim Elliot: "He is no fool who gives what he cannot keep to gain that which he cannot lose." We're to keep in mind our Savior's teaching: "Do not lay up for yourselves treasures on earth, where moth and rust destroy and where thieves break in and steal, but lay up for yourselves treasures in heaven, where neither moth nor rust destroys and where thieves do not break in and steal. For where your treasure is, there your heart will be also" (Matthew 6:19–21). Christians ought to give joyfully and generously, remembering that Jesus, "for the joy that was set before him" (Hebrews 12:2), gave everything so that we might possess all.

If we really began living generously, investing all we are and have in order to make this a better place to live for everyone, think about the witness this would be to our world. Every non-Christian around us should be able to say about us, "I might not believe what they believe, but this community would be a much less livable place without them here, because of the way these people invest their time, talents, and money in service to us." It's the fulfillment of Proverbs 11:11: "By the blessing of the upright a city is exalted."

In a world of thievery, our openhandedness just might be a more compelling witness than being able to give five rational proofs for the existence of God, as important as that is.

Real Sense

Jonathan Edwards said it's one thing to have a rational *understanding* of God's generosity and grace but quite another to have a *sense* of God's generosity and grace. How does the world genuinely encounter this sense of God's generosity and grace? Most often it's communicated through contact with God's people. We're the instruments God has equipped for that purpose.

Growing up in a wonderful Christian home, I came to know many things about God. I could repeat by heart the Apostles' Creed, the Lord's Prayer, and the Ten Commandments. But while I knew a lot about God, *I didn't know God.* What I lacked was not more and better information about God's generosity and grace but a *sense* of his generosity and a *sense* of his grace. And I received this sense as I encountered a pack of loving Christians who invested in me when there was nothing I could do for them in return. My encounter with their transformed lives helped me understand how God transforms human lives.

That's what we can do for others in our world when we become a community of givers rather than takers.

And in taking this to heart, don't overlook the most common way—and frequently the most powerful—in which we can offer something in service to others. We'll explore that next.

Redemptive Words

Because our words have power and direction, they
always produce some kind of harvest.

— PAUL TRIPP

● ● ● ● ● ●

WORDS WERE CREATED BY GOD and are a wonderful gift from him—
one that distinguishes us from animals. As John Stott says, "Cows can
moo, dogs bark, donkeys bray, pigs grunt, lambs bleat, lions roar,
monkeys squeal and birds sing, but only human beings can speak."[1]
The gift of speech is unique to those who are made in the image of
God, and it's a gift that in many ways reflects how God himself is a
communicator.

Words have always played a central role in God's plans. Words
were central in Creation, central in the Fall, and central in redemption.
In the beginning God spoke all living things into existence. In humanity's fall into sin, Satan used words to deceive Eve, Eve used words to
deceive Adam, and Adam used words to defend his disobedience and
blame Eve. Christ, our Redeemer, was himself called "the Word of
God." It was his words that brought physical and spiritual life to so
many. And it was his words from the cross—"It is finished"—that
announced his accomplishment of salvation.

God has given words tremendous value and power. But because
of sin, we abuse this gift, just as we abuse other gifts God gives us. Sex
turns into lust; money breeds greed; influence becomes oppressive
power. The tongue, says James, is ostensibly untamable. "With it we

bless our Lord and Father, and with it we curse people who are made in the likeness of God" (James 3:9). James likens the tongue to a fire (3:5–6). Just like an unrestrained fire can destroy anything in its path, so an unrestrained tongue can cause incredible damage.

That's why Paul tells us the church needs to be a community that uses the gift of speech the way God intended, as we put off hurtful words and put on helpful words: "Let no corrupting talk come out of your mouths, but only such as is good for building up, as fits the occasion, that it may give grace to those who hear" (Ephesians 4:29).

Poison or Fruit

Watching thirty minutes of political talk on television the other night, I was painfully reminded of just how easy and natural it is for people to use words to destroy, to discredit, and to discourage. I heard gossip, slander, and lies. We are all prone to misusing our God-given ability to speak by using it to serve our own ends, whatever they might be.

Think of the damage caused by the abuse of words. I've seen parent-child relationships destroyed, marriages ended, and friendships broken and never repaired, all because of the abuse of speech.

All of us have felt destroyed or discredited or discouraged by someone else's words. And all of us have destroyed and discredited and discouraged others through what we've said ourselves. Every person has to some degree felt the pain of verbal abuse. But imagine living without such sin. John Piper asks, "What would the world be like—the home, the church, the school, the public square—if words were used the way Jesus used them?"[2]

Solomon tells us, "Death and life are in the power of the tongue, and those who love it will eat its fruits" (Proverbs 18:21). In *The Message,* Eugene Peterson paraphrases the proverb like this: "Words kill, words give life; they're either poison or fruit—you choose." Words have not only destructive power but also life-giving power. They have massive potential for good and disastrous potential for evil. Our words can serve either to love or to hate, to encourage or to discourage. They have the power either to build up or tear down.

Sweetness and Strength

The church must be marked by a different language than the world exhibits, a peculiar speech. We must choose to speak *redemptively.* The sweetness and the strength of the gospel—the sweetness of grace, the strength of truth—should flavor everything we say.

In Ephesians 5:1–2, Paul tells us that we're to "be imitators of God," loving others "as Christ loved us and gave himself up for us." In our speech, as in everything else, we should be treating others the way God has treated us.

In Ephesians 2 we are reminded that Christians were once dead in sin, "children of wrath," rebelliously running from God. But in grace and mercy he sent his Son to make us "alive together with Christ" (2:1–5). Paul also tells us, in Romans 5:8, that "while we were still sinners, Christ died for us." In other words, we weren't a friend of God when he saved us; we were his enemy.

The point is, if you're a Christian, it's because God sought you and saved you—and this beautiful reality should inform the way you treat other people with your words.

Of course, since "what comes out of the mouth proceeds from the heart" (Matthew 15:18), and since "the heart is deceitful above all things, and desperately sick" (Jeremiah 17:9), our words will never be right until our hearts are put right. If our hearts are all wrong, our words will be all wrong. For our words to be filled with grace and truth, our hearts need to be filled with grace and truth.

Our only hope, then, for using words in a redemptive, God-honoring, life-giving manner is to be changed from the inside out. When we humbly submit to God's living Word, Jesus, his Spirit begins to fill our hearts with his grace and truth, and we begin to use the gift of speech the way God intended. We bring life to those who have been destroyed and discredited and discouraged by hurtful words.

Dynamics of Encouragement

Practically speaking, how should this kind of life-giving speech be demonstrated in the family of God? While there are numerous ways to use words in the manner God intended us to use them, I've come to believe that *encouragement* is the most powerful—and the most neglected.

What is encouragement?

We know it's something we all yearn for. We all know how an encouraging word from someone can carry us for weeks, months, even years. Why is that? And what is encouragement really all about?

There's a counterfeit type of encouragement and a genuine type of encouragement. The counterfeit type is what the Bible calls *flattery*. It's selfish smooth talk. The person who offers it does so for selfish reasons (*If I tell this person something nice, he'll do for me what I want him to do*). But true encouragement is different. Understood biblically, real encouragement is the verbal affirmation of someone's strength, giftedness, or accomplishment, along with the realization that God the Creator is the ultimate source behind whatever's being affirmed.

This type of encouragement is something all human beings not only crave but in fact *need*. God intended us to feed on it. The reason we require it is that we're images of God, designed to reflect him. So when others aren't acknowledging God's reflection in who we are and what we do—when we're not being encouraged—it leads to a hardened heart, a saddened disposition, and a debilitated lifestyle; we lose our sense of what it means to be human. Some of the most tragically hardened and fruitless people I know are those who have rarely, if ever, been encouraged.

The secret to true encouragement is *learning to see God's reflection in others,* not just in Christians but in everyone. Encouragement is noticing God's reflection in other people's strengths and gifts, then verbally affirming what we see. Since all human beings are made in God's image, we all—believers and unbelievers alike—reflect God in unique ways. Learning to see this uniqueness and to point it out can have a significant impact as we strive to make a difference in our world for the sake of God's kingdom.

Encouragement as Evangelism

Although we can encourage one another by our actions and attitudes, when the Bible instructs us to encourage one another, it's referring primarily to what we *say*—the words we speak. To encourage is to offer an empowering word of affirmation to others so they see God's reflection in who they are or what they've done.

Francis Schaeffer once observed that one of the best ways to evangelize people is to treat them well, and that kind of good treatment should include true encouragement. This is all the more important given the way our fast-paced, economically driven, highly technological world has numbed our sense of what it means to be human. Human beings are viewed as components in our societal machine, simply a product of random evolution with no true, inherent dignity apart from our ability to produce. What we can do and what we have are prized in our world much more than who we are.

In his book *God in the Wasteland*, David Wells discusses how the modern world and all its institutions shape the way we think about ourselves and our roles in this world. As an example, he cites the change over time in how obituaries have been written: "At the beginning of the nineteenth century, most obituaries made some mention of the character of the deceased…but by 1990 [a person's occupation] had become the key means by which a person was identified. *This substitution of function for character is a unique mark of how the modern world now understands personhood.*"[3]

But biblical encouragement reminds people that they are people.

It restores, if even for a moment, a sense of true personhood. How? Since encouraging others is the verbal affirmation of God's reflection in and through them, it awakens in them their sense of being made in God's image. It causes them to feel different, alive, profoundly human—and this helps them become aware that they're more than a number, more than a product, more than a machine, more than a chance happening. It helps them feel that they are, in fact, fearfully and wonderfully made, forcing them to reflect deeply on who they really are as human beings, which in turn causes them to reflect on their Creator. As John Calvin observed, none of us can honestly examine ourselves without coming to see that we're created *by* someone *for* someone. This recognition stirs up real humanness in people, causing them to reflect on what they're missing spiritually (not materially). They start sensing how there's more to who they are than what this world is telling them.

That's why genuine encouragement is such a powerful form of evangelism.

Shining the Light on God

The world around us struggles with encouragement. In our competitive, dog-eat-dog culture, we're pressured to be always vying for position, seeking to outdo the next person. This inevitably leads to an unwillingness to encourage. Since we know encouragement empowers people (we know this because encouragement empowers *us*), we're afraid that empowering others this way could lead to their outdoing, outshining, and outperforming us.

Regrettably, it's not much different in the church. Christians ought to know that our value rests on our union with Christ. We've been chosen by God the Father, purchased by God the Son, and sealed by God the Spirit; we're no longer slaves but children of the living God. Ultimately our value is tied not to what we do but to *whose we are,* namely God's.

I'm afraid, however, that the church tends to be just as competitive as the world. We, too, have been snookered into believing that our value is tied to our performance. We, too, try to outdo one another, fearing that our encouragement for someone will shine a light on him and take the light off us. Of course we've discovered a creative way to spiritualize our refusal to encourage.

Not long ago as I was training leaders in our church, I was reviewing my desire for New City to be an encouraging church. I explained to the men what encouragement is and how God is honored when we encourage one another.

One of the men sat back in his chair, put his hands on top of his head, and said with great relief and joy, "I've served in churches my entire adult life, and I've never heard this before. In fact, in the last church I served when I lived in California, our pastor trained those of us in leadership *not* to encourage fellow Christians because it takes the focus off of God and leads to pride." He understood for the first time that his former pastor was wrong.

By refusing to encourage others, we're actually declining to acknowledge God's reflection. In fact, to *not* give encouragement is a sin, because it amounts to a refusal to see *God,* which is the biblical definition of a fool. "The fool says in his heart, 'There is no God' " (Psalm 14:1).

Motivation for Encouragement

As Christians, we're reminded in Hebrews 10:25 to be always "encouraging one another," and the context of that exhortation gives us two compelling motivations for encouraging others.

The first is what God *has done* for us in Christ: "We have confidence to enter the holy places by the blood of Jesus, by the new and living way that he opened for us through the curtain, that is, through his flesh" (10:19–20). Jesus gives us full access to God through his bodily sacrifice—the sacrifice that pardons us from all our guilt and gives us a new mind, a new heart, a new beginning, and a clean conscience. Having thus been given everything, while deserving nothing, how could we ever be reluctant to encourage others?

Christ's self-sacrifice on the cross is the ultimate affirmation for sinners. Furthermore, he's our "great priest over the house of God" (10:21). Even now Jesus Christ is continually affirming us before God the Father. Without Christ's physical and verbal affirmation, we would be without hope in this world and the next; with it, we have "all things" (Romans 8:32). Truly understanding this cannot fail to inspire us to encourage others.

Yet there's still another reason to encourage others—what God *will do* for us in Christ. We're told to encourage others "all the more as you see the Day drawing near" (Hebrews 10:25). This "Day" is specifically the day when Christ returns and consummates his kingdom—when the new heavens and the new earth are forever established and everything wrong will forever be put right. This should motivate us to encourage both Christians and non-Christians.

It should motivate us to encourage Christians because, no matter how bad things may be, the best is yet to come. We should be verbally affirming one another's position in Christ and always reminding other Christians that we're God's children and that nothing can separate us from Christ's love. Part of our regular conversation should revolve around the permanent hope we have that one day we'll be altogether delivered from the presence of sin and will reign with Christ in a new world. We should be encouraging one another that our present pains don't compare to our future gains.

After focusing in 1 Thessalonians on this future "day of the Lord," Paul tells us, "Therefore *encourage* one another with these words" (4:18), and again, "Therefore encourage one another and build one another up" (5:11). The coming of the Lord ought to be the dominant theme of our encouragement to other believers. Christians should always be encouraging one another with the good news that Christ has been where we are and is leading us to where he now is.

On that last day God's word to his children will be "Well done, good and faithful servant" (Matthew 25:21). Isn't that interesting? God welcomes us, not by reminding us of all we failed to do or did wrong, but with a word of encouragement—the most powerful verbal affirmation we'll ever experience.

This should also motivate us to encourage non-Christians, since verbal affirmation awakens in them the realization that they're more than a cog in a machine. Encouragement stirs up real humanness in people, which causes them to reflect on who they are as creatures made in God's image. Encouraging them causes them to taste and see that they were meant to live for so much more. This is a powerful form of evangelism. And since we're closer today than we were yesterday to Christ's return, we should be all the more determined to awaken in unbelievers their critical need to become relationally connected to their Creator.

Stirring Up the "Godness"

When the writer of Hebrews speaks of our encouraging one another, he also says we're "to stir up one another to love and good works, not neglecting to meet together" (10:24–25). Here we see the effect that encouragement can have: it stirs up to love and good deeds. Encouragement is used by God to effect real change in people.

That word *stir* implies that, if you are a Christian, everything you need in order to be who God wants you to be *is already in you!* God the Holy Spirit is alive and well in you, remaking the sin-corrupted you into the person God intends you to become. He's changing you, convicting you, and maturing you. Even your deepest desires have changed as part of an internal revolution that has taken place.

A Christian's deepest desire is now for God first, not sin. In fact, each time a Christian sins, he's momentarily suffering from an identity crisis. When a Christian yields to temptation, he's living contrary to who he really is; he's being inconsistent with who he has been remade to be. He's being deceived by the flesh to think that sin, not God, is what he wants most. But even in the most intense moments of temptation, a Christian desires God more deeply than sin.

Encouragement stirs up this Godness in Christians. It reminds us of who we are, empowering us for "love and good works" (Hebrews 10:24). We often think that when a Christian messes up, what he needs most is a stern rebuke, and sometimes this is indeed necessary. (I know I need it from time to time.) But such occasional rebukes should take place in the longer-term environment of encouragement.

In fact, in the highest sense, true biblical encouragement and true biblical rebuke are rooted in the same motivations and purposes. While encouragement is verbal affirmation of God's reflection in someone, rebuke is verbal correction of the lack of God's reflection in someone. Both encouragement and rebuke are to be God-centered and motivated by love for God vertically and love for others horizontally. Encouragement moves someone from one degree of strength to another; rebuke moves someone from weakness to strength.

Community of Encouragement

This encouragement-centered passage in Hebrews 10 also makes it clear that encouragement is to be expressed first and foremost in the family of God, the church. The church is to be a community of verbal encouragement, modeling for the watching world just how freeing and empowering human life and relationships can be when there's a genuine willingness to encourage.

When God saves sinners, he saves them *as* individuals but *to* community. Isolation from other Christians is not an option for a believer. The Bible nowhere says that one can have Christ the Head without Christ the body (the church). A real relationship with God shows itself in a real relationship with his people. To neglect the body of Christ is to neglect Christ; to be isolated from the body is to be isolated from Christ.

So give yourself fully to the family of God, gladly fulfilling your call to encourage your brothers and sisters in Christ, while realizing that you'll never make it without their encouragement as well.

In Need of Improvement

So in everything we're to speak in a way that reflects how God has treated us. Therefore, it's never right to gossip, never right to slander, never right to insult. It's never right—*ever*—to hurt or discourage or to discredit or to destroy others with our words.

I think this is an area where the church needs real improvement. I talk to people all the time who have been hurt by what others in the church have said about them or to them. Gossip, slander, lies, and political maneuvering seem to be just as prevalent inside the house of God as outside. Peter reminds us, "It is time for judgment to begin at the household of God" (1 Peter 4:17)—judgment begins with us. There's no way we'll be a blessing to others on the outside, no way we'll be able to carry out God's mission, if we aren't first changed and transformed ourselves.

When we choose to speak redemptively—the way God intended—our words become a means of transforming grace. People encounter the grace of God as we give them a sense of who he is by the way we speak. You don't have to be in an evangelistic conversation for your speech to be redemptive. When you treat others with your words the way God has treated you, they'll encounter his grace regardless of what the conversation is about.

And in a world where words are so often used to destroy, this becomes a powerful exhibition of God's kingdom "on earth as it is in heaven" (Matthew 6:10).

No Longer Clammed Up

Remember there's no such thing as a small act
of kindness. Every act creates a ripple with no
logical end.

— Scott Adams

●●●●●●

The church is to be a community that puts off unkindness and puts
on kindness. That's another responsibility we have, not only individually, but as the people of God together.

But let's face it: we live in an unkind world. As I was trying to
validate this conclusion through the course of a week in preparation
for writing this chapter, I observed in detail the way people treat one
another. I watched the way people respond in traffic, what they do in
the grocery store, and how they speak to one another in public. In a
restaurant I noticed a husband degrade his wife with chauvinistic
insensitivity; at Home Depot I saw a wife disrespect her husband with
demeaning words. Closer to home, I watched our elderly neighbor
scream at our three young kids for accidentally stepping on his lawn.

I also read stories in the newspaper that illustrated just how
unkind and self-serving this world is. I read of racial violence, political dishonesty, and child prostitution. I read about a minister getting
caught for trying to solicit sex from a ten-year-old boy, and I read
about a mother who abandoned her three small children to pursue
her dream of becoming a movie star.

I really had my eyes and ears opened and saw firsthand that, while
there are many people who are kind and helpful toward others, for

the most part we live in a ruthless world. Of course this shouldn't surprise us, because the Bible tells us that the world is fallen and sinful—turned in on itself.

Every day in some form or fashion, we encounter some or all of the six things Paul identifies in Ephesians 4:31 when he writes, "Let all bitterness and wrath and anger and clamor and slander be put away from you, along with all malice." Every single day people in this world suffer the chill of unkindness. We encounter it in the workplace, on the roads, in our neighborhoods, even in our families.

What I want to show in this chapter is how clearly we impact our world for God's kingdom by rejecting those six things and choosing kindness instead. As Paul again says, "Be kind to one another, tender-hearted, forgiving one another, as God in Christ forgave you" (Ephesians 4:32).

Relationally Shut Down

Whenever there's a break in relationship between people, one or more of the evils Paul mentions—bitterness, wrath, anger, clamor, slander, and malice—is the cause. It's impossible, in fact, to find someone in this world who hasn't been damaged somehow, in some way, by these things.

And because these evils ruin relationships, they ruin community. They eventually erode even the strongest groups by breaking people down, like storm waves slamming a seaside beach.

The result of being treated in such a dehumanizing way is that most people live clammed-up lives. They've been on the receiving end of bitterness, wrath, anger, clamor, slander, or malice, and so to some degree they've shut down. Sure, they live out their lives, they go through the motions, they work and converse with people, and they do their best to engage with this world. But for the most part, they live in a perpetual state of fearful self-protection because this world and the people in it have proved to be radically unsafe and untrustworthy.

I've often counseled couples who have emotionally and physically shut down toward each other because these things have taken root in their relationship. They're afraid to give to the other—to serve each other—because they're fearful of being mistreated. They've been emotionally duped time and time again; their trust and loyalty have been abused; they've been psychologically injured by their spouse in some way. As a result they begin to live clammed-up lives with each other under the same roof.

Countless millions of people in this world live in self-protective mode all their lives. They're afraid to pour themselves out for another person, afraid to give, afraid to be vulnerable, because they're terrified of being taken.

If you stop and think about it, this is the reason our world tends to be a cold, unkind place. Our world lacks warmth because people have adopted a defensive approach to life, looking out for themselves and being suspicious of everyone else. They're refusing to give way to others, fearful that the moment they do, they'll be trampled. So they live life looking out for number one.

I have a friend whose father used to tell him that if he was ever going to make it through life unscathed, he would have to trust no one and serve only himself. And that's the way many in fact live.

Of course there are many people who seem relatively open, generous, and outgoing. But even these people are to some degree living a clammed-up life.

All this makes true, healthy, vibrant community hard to come by, whether it involves husband and wife, parents and children, neighbors, co-workers, or whatever. No relationship or community can thrive where there's bitterness and wrath and anger and clamor and slander and malice. Why? Because no relationship or community can thrive where people refuse to give of themselves.

A Better Reality

What would a world look like where there was no wrath, no slander, no malice, no self-centeredness, no bitterness? What would a community—a marriage, a family, a neighborhood, a city—look like where unkindness was nonexistent? What would a *world* look like where self-sacrifice for others and not self-protection from others marked every relationship?

Paul's instruction is that the church is to serve the world by being that type of community, where people are kind, tender-hearted, and quick to forgive. These God-dependent, gospel-driven qualities can so radically differentiate us from the culture around us that our unfashionability in these areas can take on surprising power for the kingdom.

Our mission now from God is to exhibit the realities of the age to come, when things like slander, malice, and bitterness will finally be nonexistent. But there's no way we'll be able now to faithfully carry out God's mission unless we as a community are absolutely committed to being kind, tender-hearted, and forgiving toward others.

Since I was one of seven kids—nine people in all, living together—it isn't surprising that, after John 3:16, the very next verse I was taught as a child was this one: "Be kind to one another, tenderhearted, forgiving one another, as God in Christ forgave you" (Ephesians 4:32). My mom and dad knew there was no way this rather large community all under one roof would be able to function properly and harmoniously without a radical commitment to being kind and tender-hearted and quick to forgive.

The church is to be a community that distinguishes itself by treating people well. By committing ourselves to radically distinctive kindness and forgiveness in an unkind, unforgiving world, we can make a radical difference.

A Reason for Kindness

The essential reason for treating people well should be our belief in the gospel. The gospel motivates us to treat people right by reminding us that *God in Christ has treated us right.* That's what Paul is saying in these verses: we're to be kind and tender-hearted and forgiving because God in Christ has been kind and tender-hearted and forgiving toward us.

This is cross-centered living—tracing our motivation in life back to what God in Christ has done for us. To live a cross-centered life is to treat others horizontally the way God has treated us in Christ vertically. We serve those around us because God in Christ has served us. We forgive those who wrong us because we who have wronged God (an infinitely greater offense than someone wronging us) have been forgiven by God in Christ.

Years ago I was having lunch with a pastor friend, John, who provided me with some unsolicited marriage counseling. "Tullian, after being married for over twenty-five years, I've come to realize that the phrase 'easy marriage' is an oxymoron. The bottom line is that sometimes your wife will be unkind, and when she is, you'll be tempted to conclude in those moments that she doesn't deserve your kindness, your forgiveness. When this temptation has happened to me in the past, God has reminded me very quickly that while I was unlovely, unkind, and running away from God's love, Christ gave himself up for me. Jesus displayed infinite kindness, tender-heartedness, and forgiveness toward me when I least deserved it."

Both Kim and I have hung on to John's wise counsel for years now. It has helped to remind us, not only of the importance of being kind, tender-hearted, and forgiving toward each other, but also of the way we need to act toward those around us who aren't this way.

Cross-centered living requires us to remember that Christ laid his life down for God's enemies, not for his friends. Each of us comes into this world, as Paul tells us in Ephesians 2, as a child of wrath, an enemy of God. But "God shows his love for us in that while we were still sinners, Christ died for us" (Romans 5:8). The fact that we've been eternally loved and accepted by God is a mark of his unconditional grace, and our lives ought therefore to be marked by the same unconditional grace.

Everything I Need, I Have

Think about how freeing this is. Having received all the kindness and tender-heartedness and forgiveness we need from God, we become free to give to others without risk, because our deepest needs have already been fully met in Christ.

For example, while I may enjoy kindness from my wife, I don't "need" it. In Jesus I receive all the kindness I need. This enables me to be kind to her without the fear that she might not return the favor. I get to revel in her enjoyment of my kindness without needing that kindness to be reciprocated. I *get* kindness from Christ so that I can *give* kindness to her.

When you multiply that freedom across every relationship you have, you're liberated to lay down your life for other people (especially your enemies) without needing anything from them in return, because in Christ you've been given everything you need. This liberates you from living a clammed-up life in fearful self-protection.

Living out this reality would transform our relationships with our spouse, kids, neighbors, co-workers—everyone. Most important, it would transform this world. As we become a community that devotes itself to being kind and tender-hearted and forgiving, we warm up this cold world, making it more livable for everyone. We show this world how freeing, safe, warm, and secure life can be when it's marked by tender-heartedness and kindness and forgiveness—when it's marked by the gospel.

We make a difference by treating people differently. The church is to be a community that puts off unkindness and puts on kindness.

Love, Not Lust

I'm stranded in the wrong time
where love is just a lyric
in a children's rhyme.

— KEANE

●●●●●●

SEVERAL CHAPTERS AGO WE LEARNED that the apostle Paul laid out six defining marks that ought to identify the community of God. These are ways that we, as the body of Christ, can become beautifully unfashionable in this world. So far, from Ephesians 4, we've found that we are to...

- put off lying and put on truthfulness,
- put off self-centered anger and put on God-centered anger,
- put off stealing and put on generosity,
- put off hurtful speech and put on redemptive speech,
- put off bitterness, wrath, anger, clamor, slander, and malice and put on kindness.

Finally we turn the page to Ephesians 5 and discover one more put-off, put-on characteristic of the unfashionable church. And given the nature of our present culture, this characteristic may be the most important of them all. The church is to be a community that puts off sexual immorality and puts on love.

Paul has a lot to say about this:

Be imitators of God, as beloved children. And walk in love, as Christ loved us and gave himself up for us, a fragrant offering and sacrifice to God.

But sexual immorality and all impurity or covetousness must not even be named among you, as is proper among saints. Let there be no filthiness nor foolish talk nor crude joking, which are out of place, but instead let there be thanksgiving. For you may be sure of this, that everyone who is sexually immoral or impure, or who is covetous (that is, an idolater), has no inheritance in the kingdom of Christ and God. (Ephesians 5:1–5)

My friend Josh wrote a book with a great title: *Sex Is Not the Problem (Lust Is)*. In it he shows that God has created us as sexual beings and that sex is, in fact, a gift from God that he intends for us to enjoy in the context of a loving relationship between husband and wife. In this context sex becomes the ultimate expression of God's intimate love for us.

But as I mentioned earlier, we often abuse God's gifts. We take the good gifts God gives us, and we twist them and pervert them. In so doing we turn something meant to help us into something that ultimately hurts us. And that's especially true when it comes to sex and lust.

What I want to show in this chapter is how choosing love over lust can effect a radical influence for God's kingdom in our world.

Lonely Culture

There's no doubt we live in a lust-saturated world. Every day we're bombarded by the sexual objectification of human beings. Both men and women are constantly being sold to the consumer as objects for self-indulgence. In our sexualized culture, billions of dollars are spent every year on pornography, "an industry that enslaves countless people to the vice of voyeurism and perverts the normal expectations of sexual expression between men and women in marriage."[1] Sex is used to sell just about everything from homes to cars, cologne, beer, and clothes. Sexual promiscuity is romanticized and celebrated as the means to true freedom and the ultimate expression of one's right to personal pleasure.

Youth culture is more than ever saturated with the fashionability of lust and sexual licentiousness. From the explicit pictures of Abercrombie & Fitch catalogs, to the half-naked teenage employees who wait on you at Hollister Co., to virtually every reality show on TV and every pop song on the radio, the message is the same: sexual promiscuity is stylish; sacrificial love is overrated.

But however progressive and cool it may look on the surface, the posture of promiscuity is actually the sad concession of a deeply lonely culture.

In a recent talk given at a Christian college, journalist Andy Crouch showed the connection between sexual promiscuity and the rapid rise of binge drinking among college-age women, 40 percent of whom have had more than four drinks in a row in the last week, according to a survey. "I have a theory about this," Crouch said. "I believe that drinking for college-age women is largely a way to make sex easier—to ease the pain of hooking up, the pain of anonymous sex. Sex with someone you've made no promises to, for whom you haven't changed your name, is indeed anonymous, without-a-name sex. It's also story-less sex, with no history and no future. When it stops feeling good, it hurts, because sex is made to change our names, to change our stories. And when it doesn't change us, it leaves us empty and lost, stranded outside the story we were made to live in."[2]

Andy's words show that underneath our culture's fascination with sexual promiscuity and lust is a deeper, unsatisfied desire for a more meaningful and long-lasting form of relational intimacy. Because the modern world is always changing and never staying the same, millions of people feel disconnected and alone.

It shouldn't surprise us, for instance, that the meteoric rise in teenage pregnancies is happening at the same time our culture is becoming increasingly dependent on modern telecommunications. Technology connects us broadly with others but not deeply, and this lack of deep relationships creates an uncomfortable anonymity that makes people desperate to find relational intimacy anywhere and any way they can. And since real love—name-changing, story-changing love—seems hopelessly out of reach (existing only in fairy tales), people settle for what they believe is the next best thing: hooking up. Thinking they can find satisfaction to their hunger for deep relational connection in and through sexual encounters, they become promiscuous—if not physically, then virtually (hence the rise in the use of Internet pornography and sexual chat rooms). Millions of people jump from bed to bed and chat room to chat room, trying desperately to scratch a deep itch that commitment-free sex simply can't reach.

Promiscuity promises what it cannot give. We need something bigger, something deeper.

The Real Problem with Sexual Sin

Responding to the youth culture's fascination with hooking up, many well-meaning organizations have developed abstinence courses intended to discourage sexual promiscuity. But as well intentioned as abstinence educators might be, they miss the real problem.

In an article entitled "Scaring the Sex out of You," John Seel writes about listening to an abstinence presentation in his church.

> Sex outside of marriage, I was told, can destroy your dreams. What teenager wants to be saddled with raising a baby? Only those who abstain from sex, we were admonished, will find success and freedom. The bulk of the presentation was a detailed description of the 25 different types of sexually transmitted diseases and how condoms and other forms of

contraceptives are not 100% reliable protection from symp-
toms ranging from infertility (chlamydia) to death (AIDS).
Alas, abstinence education often boils down to fear monger-
ing. It's a veiled attempt to scare the sex out of you.[3]

The real problem with sexual sin that John is getting at is not sexually transmitted diseases or unwanted pregnancies. Those are the fruit
of a much deeper problem. The real problem with sexual sin is that it
dehumanizes and cheapens people. Sexual sin treats other people as
commodities, objects to possess. It causes us to view another person as
being there for us to take, not as someone to serve, and that is a radical departure from what God intends our relationships to be.

Sexual sin is always treated more seriously than other sins in the
Bible because it violates what God values most in creation: human
beings made in his image. When we indulge in sexual sin, we denigrate
the reflection of God. We treat with contempt what God has deemed
most dignified.

That's why Paul tells us in Ephesians 5 that we shouldn't make
light of sexual immorality. Because God views it so seriously, we should
never joke about sexual sin.

Afraid of Love

Our culture's dismissal of sacrificial, long-term love in favor of sexual
sin is understandable from one perspective. True love, while not out
of reach, *is* downright scary. In *The Four Loves,* C. S. Lewis writes, "To
love at all is to be vulnerable. Love anything, and your heart will certainly be wrung and possibly be broken. If you want to make sure of
keeping it intact, you must give your heart to no one, not even an animal."[4] Lewis wasn't saying we should avoid love but instead was simply making the observation that real love is risky; it opens one up to
the possibility of intense emotional ache. In fact, Lewis says, the only
place outside of heaven where one can be perfectly safe from all the

dangers of love is hell, and that's because love is altogether absent there.

But Lewis goes on to make the point that this risk is worth it because true love, as evidenced at the cross of Christ, is driven not by self-preservation but self-sacrifice. Love, as the Bible defines it, is sacrificial.

This, however, threatens our natural tendency to protect ourselves. We're afraid to give because we're afraid of being taken. But this self-centered fear is precisely why we so often miss out on true love and settle instead for sexual sin. We've come to believe that love is first something we *get* from others before it's something we *give* others.

But as someone once said, love is what exists between people who find their joy in each other's joy. The real benefit of true love comes from loving others before it comes from being loved. Therefore, to give is to receive—not the other way around. Sexual sin misses deep intimacy because it's all about self-gratification, not self-sacrifice.

Captivating Love

The gospel is the reason why the church is to be a community that embodies and exhibits true self-giving love in a sexually promiscuous, lust-saturated world.

In 1970 Francis Schaeffer wrote an essay called "The Mark of the Christian," in which he argued that love is the Christian's fundamental characteristic. He grounded his conclusion in the words of Jesus in John 13:34–35: "A new commandment I give to you, that you love one another: just as I have loved you, you also are to love one another. By this all people will know that you are my disciples, if you have love for one another." Likewise Paul tells us that the church is to "walk in love." Why? Because Christ "loved us and gave himself up for us" (Ephesians 5:2). The apostle John underscored the same point when he wrote, "By this we know love, that he [Christ] laid down his life for us, and we ought to lay down our lives for the brothers" (1 John 3:16).

In a world that cheapens people by objectifying them, dehumanizing them, and viewing them as commodities meant to serve our needs instead of as persons for us to serve, Christians are to demonstrate that real love is *not* out of reach, that in the person of Christ true love has in fact reached down to us, and that this love is, without question, more enchanting, more substantive, and more satisfying than promiscuity. It is name-changing, story-changing love. It's not anonymous, and it's not commitment free. It is real, deep, and covenant keeping.

> Love is patient and kind; love does not envy or boast; it is
> not arrogant or rude. It does not insist on its own way; it is
> not irritable or resentful; it does not rejoice at wrongdoing,
> but rejoices with the truth. Love bears all things, believes all
> things, hopes all things, endures all things.
> Love never ends. (1 Corinthians 13:4–8)

We're to show our lonely world just how much more captivating and satisfying loving self-sacrifice is in comparison to sexual self-indulgence. We're to show that there's an immeasurable difference between sexual lust and self-giving love: one seeks to use people, while the other seeks to serve people; one tears people down, while the other builds people up.

We need to demonstrate for the world what human community can look like when people serve one another instead of use one another, when people find joy in each other's joy. That's what love is.

In all the long history of Christians who have been rescued from captivity to sexual lust, the story of Augustine in the fifth century is one of the most profound. In John Piper's biography of the great churchman and theologian, he reminds us of how Augustine from early manhood lived a life "utterly given over to sexual pleasures," and his battle with lust consumed him for years, even as he made intellectual progress toward belief in Christ, and his mind and heart warmed toward the Lord's attractiveness. As Piper summarizes the struggle, Augustine was asking, "How shall I find strength to enjoy God more than sex?"[5]

One day the intensity of his long struggle reached a peak, plunging him into agony. Almost miraculously he was led to Paul's words in Romans 13:13–14: "Let us walk properly as in the daytime, not in orgies and drunkenness, not in sexual immorality and sensuality, not in quarreling and jealousy. But put on the Lord Jesus Christ, and make no provision for the flesh, to gratify its desires." In that moment God's Spirit opened his entire life and soul to the truth. Suddenly, as Augustine himself describes it, "I had no wish to read more and no need to do so. For in an instant, as I came to the end of the sentence, it was as though the light of confidence flooded into my heart and all the darkness of doubt was dispelled."[6] This passionate man became a tireless, passionate lover of God's church and God's truth. In faithfully serving his generation, he became a spiritual giant already in his own time and has remained one for all of history. For a thousand years Augustine's influence was unequaled as the champion of the power of grace over bondage to sin.

As a result of our putting true love on display for the entire world to see, lost and lonely people will know there's something different about us—and it *will* make a difference, just as it did for Augustine.

Part 4

The Charge

Last Call

Who stands fast?... The responsible man who tries
to make his whole life an answer to the question and
call of God. Where are these responsible people?

— DIETRICH BONHOEFFER

●●●●●●

BOTH THE BIBLE AND HISTORY bear witness to the fact that it's not so much big churches or big ministries that have the most impact in our world; it's big Christians. And I don't mean those whose physical stature resembles that of Hulk Hogan. I mean those whose spiritual stature resembles that of Polycarp, bishop of Smyrna in the second century, when the Roman emperor Marcus Aurelius had ordered the persecution of all Christians.

The story of how Polycarp handled his persecution is, for me, one of the greatest examples of big Christianity this world has ever known. John Foxe, in his famous work, *Foxe's Christian Martyrs of the World*, tells the story best:

Hearing his captors had arrived one evening, Polycarp left his bed to welcome them, ordered a meal prepared for them, and then asked for an hour alone to pray. The soldiers were so impressed by Polycarp's advanced age and composure that they began to wonder why they had been sent to take him, but as soon as he had finished his prayers, they put him on a donkey and brought him to the city.

Brought before the tribunal and the crowd, Polycarp refused to deny Christ, although the proconsul begged him to "consider yourself and have pity on your great age. Reproach Christ and I will release you."

Polycarp replied, "Eighty-six years I have served Him, and He has never once wronged me. How can I blaspheme my King, who saved me?"

Threatened with wild beasts and fire, Polycarp stood his ground. "What are you waiting for? Do whatever you please." The crowd demanded Polycarp's death, gathering wood for the fire and preparing to tie him to the stake. "Leave me," he said. "He who will give me strength to sustain the fire will help me not to flinch from the pile." So they bound him but didn't nail him to the stake.

As soon as Polycarp finished his prayer, the fire was lit, but it leaped up around him, leaving him unburned, until the people convinced a soldier to plunge a sword into him. When he did, so much blood gushed out that the fire was extinguished. The soldiers then placed his body into a fire and burned it to ashes, which some Christians later gathered up and buried properly.[1]

Every time I read that account, I get shivers up my spine. And I'm reminded of how desperately the world today needs more Christians like him.

Because religious freedom in most parts of the world is protected, many of us will never face the physical danger Polycarp endured because of his commitment to Jesus. Most of us don't have to fear being put to death or placed in prison for our faith in Jesus. But we face danger of another, more toxic sort. Jesus said, "Do not be afraid of that which can kill the body but be afraid of that which can kill the soul" (see Matthew 10:28). While we must never forget the physical suffering of our Christian brothers and sisters in places like Southeast

Asia, Africa, and China, we must keep in mind that the greatest threat to a thriving, God-saturated, world-transforming faith is not physical danger but worldliness.

Worldliness, as I described earlier, is a sleepiness of the soul in which the status, pleasures, comforts, and cares of the world appear solid, stunning, and affecting, while the truths of Scripture become abstractions—unable to grip the heart or guide our everyday activities. This means that the greatest challenge facing most Christians is not persecution but seduction.

Becoming "all things to all people" (1 Corinthians 9:22) does *not* mean fitting in with the fallen patterns of this world so that there's no distinguishable difference between Christians and non-Christians. When this world's sin patterns start to seem normal and God's ways start to seem strange, we know we've been seduced. When this happens, Christians become miserably ineffective.

The point I've made repeatedly in this book is that we transform this world by being distinct from it, living *against* the world *for* the world. That means, of course, that the opposite is true too—we fail to make a difference in the world when we fail to be different from the world.

Culture Shock

I have friends who are foreign missionaries, and they tell me that one of the hardest things to get used to as a missionary is culture shock. It happens when they arrive in a foreign field or return home after being away for a long time. It's caused when one set of cultural assumptions clashes with another set, when what seems normal to them in one cultural setting seems uncomfortably strange in another. After a couple of months, however, the culture shock goes away. Over time they gradually settle into the assumptions and behavioral patterns of the culture around them. As one of them told me, "Shock eventually gives way to submission."

Culture shock has always been a helpful image to me as I try to understand the challenge of living in the world but not being of the world. In the case of missionaries coming back home or arriving in a foreign field, the sooner culture shock wears off, the better. But there's a deeper level of culture shock that *all* Christians, regardless of where they live or what they do, must never allow to wear off. *Faithfully following Christ requires that Christians maintain a constant state of culture shock in relation to the sinful patterns of the world.* As followers of Jesus, we must maintain what psychologists call "cognitive dissonance" toward the patterns of culture that undermine our loyalty to God and his unfashionable ways. For Christians to embody a vibrant, world-transforming presence in our culture, shock must never give way to submission; tension *with* the world must never give way to comfort *in* the world. My fear, however, is that it already has for many professing Christians.

How many of us, for example, under the intense pressure to give in and go along, possess the spiritual backbone to face social scorn and contempt the way Polycarp did? How many of us quickly renounce allegiance to our King and the unfashionable way he has called us to think and live just so we'll fit in and be culturally accepted?

As I examine the spiritual stature of many professing Christians in our day, including my own, I wonder, *Where are the Polycarps today?* I see plenty of big churches and big ministries, but where are all the big Christians? Are there many Christians left who are willing to die, physically or socially, for God's unfashionable ways? Are there many Christians left who are willing and desiring to leave it all on the field for Christ's sake?

Remember that Jesus never went looking for crowds; he went looking for disciples. And to get disciples, he explained that any who wanted to follow him would need to count the cost. Daily Christian living, according to Jesus, means daily Christian dying—dying to our fascination with fitting in and instead joyfully becoming a "fool for Christ."

My suspicion is that if all Christians were similar in spiritual stature to Polycarp, the Christian witness in this world would be much greater than it is. It took only twelve God-intoxicated men, full of the Holy Spirit, to turn the world upside down (see Acts 17:6, KJV)—or, more accurately, right side up! As E. M. Bounds said famously, "Men are God's method. The church is looking for better methods; God is looking for better men."[2]

Better men and women would be big Christians who never get over their culture shock in this world, because they refuse to give up the ways of God in favor of the world's ways.

Remembering God

The seed for this book was planted in me fourteen years ago as I was sitting in an upstairs cubicle in my college library reading David Wells's book *God in the Wasteland.* In it Wells meticulously shows that God rests too lightly, too inconsequentially, on the modern church: "His truth is too distant, his grace is too ordinary, his judgment is too benign, his Gospel is too easy, and his Christ is too common."[3] All the bells and whistles in the church have caused us to forget the God whose church it is. We've become entirely too comfortable with the ways and tastes of this world, and it has led to our increasing irrelevance—we're failing to make a difference because we're failing to be different.

I'll never forget the morning I came to the end of *God in the Wasteland* and read the following paragraph. I don't think it's an overstatement for me to say that, outside the Bible, no paragraph ever written motivates me more or captures my hope better than this one from Wells. It has become my impassioned plea to young evangelicals:

> I want the evangelical church to be the church. I want it to
> embody a vibrant spirituality. I want the church to be an
> alternative to post-modern culture, not a mere echo of it. I

want a church that is bold to be different and unafraid to be
faithful,…a church that reflects an integral and undimin-
ished confidence in the power of God's Word, a church that
can find in the midst of our present cultural breakdown the
opportunity to be God's people in a world that has abandoned God. To be the church in this way, it is also going to
have to find in the coming generation, leaders who exemplify this hope for its future and who will devote themselves
to seeing it realized…. They will have to decline to spend
themselves in the building of their own private kingdoms
and refuse to be intimidated into giving the church less and
other than what it needs…. To succeed, they will have to be
people of large vision, people of courage, people who have
learned again what it means to live by the Word of God,
and, most importantly, what it means to live before the Holy
God of that Word.[4]

To the degree that God becomes relevant once again in the life of
the church, so that God's truth, and not social trends, becomes the
driving force behind everything we are and do, the church will become
what the world needs it to be—a counterculture for the common
good.

Becoming a Fool for Christ

But this is the problem: many Christians seem just as fascinated with
success, popularity, power, and prestige as the world around them.
Materialism, consumerism, individualism, and narcissism—cultural
ideals that are antithetical to the self-sacrificial nature of the gospel—
are just as prevalent inside the church as they are outside. *The sad fact
is that we in the American church are better known for producing self-
exalting superstars than self-sacrificial servants.*

If professing Christians took an honest inventory of our own pursuits and the desires that motivate them (even if on the surface they seem God honoring), we would discover that we're really no different from the world around us. Therefore, we have no right to point the finger at those outside the church for the way things are in this world. Many studies show that Christians are almost indistinguishable from non-Christians in their pursuit of fame and fortune, clout and cachet. Christians want to fit in just like everyone else. So we, just like everyone else, spend our time, our money, and our intellectual energy chasing after what everyone else is chasing after, whatever that might be.

Here's the bottom line: *I* want to be a big Christian, and I want *you* to be a big Christian. I want the church to be filled with people like Polycarp. Polycarp was a God-drenched man; I want to be a God-drenched man. Every part of Polycarp's being was devoted to God and his unfashionable ways. Nothing else could explain his God-centered perspective during the most trying time of his life. He refused to give in and go along. To him, following God was no joke and no popularity contest. He was a God-intoxicated man who lived his life *coram Deo* (before the face of God) and who was therefore unafraid of anything this world could do to him.

I don't know about you, but I don't want to play around with my life. I want to leave it all out on the field for Christ's sake. I don't want to be a mile wide and an inch deep spiritually. I want to possess the backbone to dig in and be unfashionable. I'm ashamed of those moments when I'm afraid to be a fool for Christ because the world might think I'm strange. I want to have a God-given, uncommon valor to follow God's lead and do God's will, regardless of how I might be perceived. I want to live my life, as the Puritans used to say, before "an audience of One."

Christians who try to convince the world around them that they're really no different at all, hoping they'll be accepted on the world's terms and on the world's turf, should be embarrassed. It's time for Christians to embrace the fact that we're peculiar people. Because true followers of Jesus have been given a new heart and mind, we're to operate according to a different standard, with different goals and motivations. Everything about us—our perspective on possessions, lifestyle, and relationships—will be foundationally different from the world around us: "We worship what we cannot see, love what we cannot hold, and live for what we cannot own." To the world around us, this will seem out of place, uncool, and odd; it's high time followers of Jesus learn to embrace that fact.

Thankfully, some have.

I just read a news story today about three men who were punished by officials in Shaanxi Province in China. While their women were forced to watch, the three men were beaten until they were covered with blood and gaping wounds. Then the officers hung them up naked and began hitting their backs with rods until the three were unconscious and barely breathing.

The victims were Christians. Their crime was unapologetically communicating the unfashionable truth of the gospel to foreigners.

The Bible tells us exactly what it takes to become—as these three were—big Christians who make a big difference. It takes learning how to identify worldliness and resolving to be weaned from it. This requires being absolutely sure that this world in its present fallen state, with all of its present fallen tastes, is not our home. No one could face unjust suffering with the bravery that Polycarp did unless he knew God's ways were higher and better than the world's ways. Polycarp was able to joyfully accept undeserved physical and social misery because he knew, like the Christians addressed in Hebrews 10:34, that he had "a better possession and an abiding one." He knew that "here we have no lasting city," so he sought "the city that is to come" (Hebrews 13:14). He was able to stand firm when he felt the heat, because he believed that "the world is passing away along with its desires, but whoever does the will of God abides forever" (1 John 2:17). Polycarp's bold otherworldliness enabled him to shamelessly embrace God's unfashionable ways in the hour of temptation—that hour when giving in would have been easier than digging in.

In this fallen world every follower of Christ should expect that our captors will arrive. After all, Jesus told his disciples that since the world hated him, it would hate them too (see John 15:18). And the only thing that will keep us standing firm when social pressure and persecution arrive at our door is knowing that we belong to a King whose kingdom is not of this world (see John 18:36).

There's just no other way to stand our ground as Polycarp did when "threatened with wild beasts and fire." There's no other way to give our utmost for Christ's sake than to be sure that our ultimate citizenship lies in the city that is to come.

Our Unfashionable Trailblazer

In a world that's decidedly anti-God, following God's unfashionable ways can be wearisome, scary, trying, and intimidating. On top of this external pressure from the world is the reality that all of us desperately long for acceptance. In fact, we spend the better part of our lives trying to be approved, to be liked. We think life will become more meaningful—that we'll *be* somebody—to the degree that we can get in with the right person or the right group. If we can achieve a certain level of worldly success, we'll be accepted by those around us; people will conclude that we matter, that we're important.

I encountered this with one of my boys recently.

My boys love football. They have the skill for it, the heart for it, and the mind for it. But like their dad, at this point they don't have the body for it. And sometimes that really gets to them. They're afraid they won't be big enough to play the game. One of them was really upset about this recently, and so we talked. I went up to his room, where he was crying, and said, "I know this may seem deeper than you want to go right now, but this is what's really causing you to be upset: you've come to believe that you don't matter—that you'll never be accepted—if you don't succeed in sports. And you think that your success in sports depends on your size. This means you're depending on your physical development to give you significance. You think acceptance depends on your size."

What I told him is also what I have to daily remind myself of and what I tell you now: In and of itself, your longing for acceptance isn't a bad thing. God, in fact, created you for acceptance. This longing, however, was meant to be satisfied by God alone. But because of sin, we look to things smaller than God for it—things incapable of providing the infinite approval we crave. Your deep longing for acceptance can be satisfied only when you're accepted by the One who made you for himself. If you embrace what Christ has done on the cross for sinners, you're in! Your infinite hunger for approval will be forever satisfied, because you'll be unchangeably accepted by the only One who offers eternal acceptance. You'll no longer have to depend on finite things like your size, your stuff, or your smarts to get you in so that your life will matter. Once you understand that in Christ you're accepted by God, you're free and empowered to live unfashionably, because you won't need the acceptance of the world around you. You won't care if you're in with them, because you'll already be in with *him*.

We can also take great comfort in the fact that, because we're united to Christ, all that is his (humanly speaking) is ours. He has made it possible for us to be the unfashionable people God designed us to be.

In his book *Grow in Grace,* Sinclair Ferguson reflects on the fact that Jesus is the captain of our salvation and the pioneer of our faith. He has beaten down a path for us to follow. Because Christ loved and lived God's unfashionable ways, we can love and live God's unfashionable ways too. Because Christ dug down deep and stood against the pressures of this world, we can dig down deep and stand against the pressures of this world too. He's our great trailblazer, our divine bushwhacker. Ferguson provides this vivid illustration:

> Picture an army captain hacking his way through a jungle
> during a battle with guerrilla forces. He leads his men from
> danger to safety by first facing the dangers, impediments,

and tests himself. Similarly, Jesus is the Captain of our salvation. He has not only tasted all of our experiences of temptation but he has gone further. He experienced them in their full strength, when they unleashed all their powers against him. Where we would stumble and fall, he has pressed on. He overcame temptation, conquered death and drew its sting. Now he beckons us: "Follow me, the pathway of faith is trustworthy for all of you to use!"[5]

Our unfashionable Leader has promised that, because he has already done it, we can now do it.

Christians throughout history have believed this in their most trying moments, when the temptation to give in and give up was strongest.

Robert Glover was a devout follower of Christ in England. In 1555 he was arrested for denying state-approved doctrine, tried for heresy, and sentenced to burn at the stake. Just days before his execution, Robert experienced a sense of God's dreadful withdrawal, and he fell into despair, fearing that God had abandoned his soul. One of Robert's friends, Austin, visited him in prison and encouraged him to stay patient and wait for God, saying that God would come back before the end.

The day before his death, Robert spent most of his time in prayer, but he still felt no presence or comfort from God. The next day, however, as his executioners led him to the stake, he suddenly felt God's presence so profoundly that he started clapping his hands in joy and crying out, "Oh, Austin, he has come! He has come!"

When the pressure to give in and go along seems unbearable, we can bank on our Savior, who has promised never to leave us or forsake us.

To us he has given—and will continue to give—grace and truth. And it's grace enough and truth enough that we'll become people who make a profound difference in this world…by being profoundly different from this world.

A Reading List: Unriddling Our Times

We've seen how the Bible makes clear that Christians must be people of double listening—listening both to the questions of the world and to the answers of the Word. We're to be good interpreters not only of Scripture but also of culture. God wants us to be like the men of Issachar, "who had understanding of the times, to know what Israel ought to do" (1 Chronicles 12:32). Faithfulness to Christ means we can't afford to leave our culture unexamined. We're to think long and hard, deep and wide about our times and all the issues surrounding the church's mission—its proper relationship *to* this world and its proper place *in* it.

I don't claim to understand all of the complexities involved and the challenges that face Christians in different parts of the world, but I would like to offer some direction regarding what I consider must-read books that can help us think through these issues biblically. No one will agree with all of the content in these books. In fact, some of these books represent opposing perspectives on how Christians should relate to the culture around them. But all of these books will help you develop your own conclusions.

As I once heard Tim Keller say, "Read one thinker and you become a clone. Read two and you become confused. Read a hundred and you start to become wise." While I don't list a hundred books here, these are my Top 40, and I'm convinced they'll help you on that road to wisdom. All these books are well written, but none of them is easy reading. They all require an engaged mind. I know this sounds crazy, but I suggest that over time you try to read them all.

I also urge you to be a diligent and intentional reader. Highlight and underline key phrases and sentences, and make notes in the margins. As C. S. Lewis said, "The best way to read is with book in lap, pen in hand, and pipe in teeth." So enjoy these books—but easy on the tobacco.

Here are my top fifteen recommendations:

American Evangelicalism by James Davison Hunter

Chameleon Christianity by Dick Keyes

Christ and Culture Revisited by D. A. Carson

Christian Mission in the Modern World by John Stott

Culture Making by Andy Crouch

Engaging God's World by Cornelius Plantinga

God in the Wasteland by David Wells

The Gospel in a Pluralist Society by Lesslie Newbigin

The Gravedigger File by Os Guinness

How Now Shall We Live? by Chuck Colson and Nancy Pearcey

Lectures on Calvinism by Abraham Kuyper

No Place for Truth, or, Whatever Happened to Evangelical Theology? by David Wells

Resident Aliens by Stanley Hauerwas and William Willimon

The Way of the Modern World by Craig Gay

Where in the World Is the Church? by Michael Horton

And here are twenty-five more I highly recommend:

The Abolition of Man by C. S. Lewis

All God's Children and Blue Suede Shoes by Ken Myers

Christ and Culture by H. Richard Niebuhr

The Church Before the Watching World by Francis Schaeffer

The Contemporary Christian by John Stott

Creation Regained by Albert Wolters

The Culturally Savvy Christian by Dick Staub

Culture Matters by T. M. Moore

He Shines in All That's Fair by Richard Mouw

Heaven Is a Place on Earth by Michael E. Wittmer

Heaven Is Not My Home by Paul Marshall

Making the Best of It by John G. Stackhouse Jr.

No God but God by John Seel and Os Guinness

The Noise of Solemn Assemblies by Peter Berger

Not the Way It's Supposed to Be by Cornelius Plantinga

A Peculiar People by Rodney Clapp

Prophetic Untimeliness by Os Guinness

Redeeming Pop-Culture by T. M. Moore

A Rumor of Angels by Peter Berger

Surprised by Hope by N. T. Wright

The Transforming Vision by Brian Walsh and Richard Middleton

Too Christian, Too Pagan by Dick Staub

Total Truth by Nancy Pearcey

When the Kings Come Marching In by Richard Mouw

Where Resident Aliens Live by Stanley Hauerwas and William Willimon

Study Guide for Personal and Gr●up Use

Chapter 1. A Cry for Difference

After discovering the emptiness of a life lived for worldly pleasure, the author—Tullian Tchividjian—was confronted by a high and lifted-up God who was being celebrated by a group of Christians whose lives were radically different from what he knew. Today, as a pastor, he reflects on the importance of that kind of witness. In chapter 1 he says, "The point I want to drive home in this book is this: *Christians make a difference in this world by being different from this world; they don't make a difference by being the same.*"

1. What was your reason for picking up this book to read? What were you hoping to get out of it?

2. When have you encountered a Christian group or church that was so radically different from the world that it caught your attention and made you think about God in a new way?

3. When have you encountered a Christian group or church that was so similar to the world that it roused little interest?

4. Read Hebrews 11. How does this catalog of faithful men and women reveal that God's people ought to expect to feel like foreigners in the world?

5. "Christians make a difference in this world by being different from this world; they don't make a difference by being the same." To what extent do you agree or disagree? What questions do you have about how this concept plays out in real life?

Chapter 2. A World Without Windows

The author says our world's rationalism and materialism have given people a hunger for the supernatural. And so, while many Christians are working hard to fit in to the world and appear hip and up-to-date, that's not what many unbelievers want. They're looking for genuine truth and transcendence. They're looking for people with a real connection to God, regardless of how off-center it is from today's fads or fashions.

1. Thinking back over the last twenty-four hours, what is one way you have seen our world's prevailing rationalistic outlook expressed? What is one way you have seen a countervailing yearning for the sacred or the supernatural?

2. How have you seen Christians try to be relevant by copying what is "in" at the moment?

3. How have you seen unbelievers react to Christians' attempts to be relevant?

4. Read Acts 2. How does it highlight the difference between power and production in a faith community that was distinctively different?

5. The author describes the real path to meeting people's need for God this way: "When the size of God grips us more than the size of our churches and leadership conferences, and when we become obsessed with surrendering our lives to God's sovereign presence, only then will we be redemptively different and serve as God's cosmic change agents in a world yearning for change." What's your reaction to that?

Chapter 3. Seduced by Cool

If we're to believe the founder of our faith, Christianity is not supposed to be cool. Jesus's way is a hard and uncomfortable way that bears little resemblance to the "good life" glamorized in entertainment media and advertising. Yet many Christians, having been "seduced by cool," are imitating the world's image of how one is supposed to live. The reality is, while we're supposed to love the *world,* we have to divorce ourselves from *worldliness* if we're going to live for Jesus with any effectiveness.

1. Think about Jesus's ministry. How did he *not* fit in with the world in terms of his lifestyle? his companions? his teaching? his interactions with people in power? his death?
2. Read 1 Corinthians 1–3. What is the world's "wisdom," and why is it really foolish? What is the "foolishness" of Jesus, and why is it really wise?
3. As the author defines it, what is the difference between the world's structure and its direction? What relevance does this have for how Christians are to behave?
4. How can Christians be culturally *aware* but not culturally *entangled*?
5. How is your conscience convicting you about being too fashionable?

Chapter 4. An Unfashionable Standard

The world sees each of us as in charge of determining what we are going to believe and how we are going to live; it doesn't accept transcendent truth from God. Even many professing Christians, it's sad to say, are reluctant to live by the Bible when it comes right down to it. But God means for the Bible to guide our whole lives, forming our attitudes toward both him and ourselves. And this is how we become distinctively Christian—unfashionable.

1. Think of two or three unbelievers you know well. What do they think about truth—is it absolute or relative? What is their attitude toward the Bible?

2. What evidence have you seen that Tullian is right when he says that many professing Christians accept the Bible's authority only up to a point?

3. How have you, personally, been reluctant to let the teachings of the Bible judge or change you?

4. Read Hebrews 4:12. How does it describe the effect that the Word of God has had in your life?

5. "When the relevance of God's Word reigns supreme among God's set-apart people," says Tullian, "we influence the wider culture by expressing his revealed truth with both our lives and our lips." Do you agree that the Bible is the key to our influence? Why or why not?

Chapter 5. The Purpose-Driven Death

What motivates us to live unfashionably? It's the grand story told by the Bible, an arc of meaning stretching from Creation through the Fall to redemption. In particular, it's important for us to understand that God is in the process of redeeming all things—not just individual human souls, but also communities, cultures, and the earth itself. So we shouldn't think of ourselves as just hanging on until we can escape this world. We're supposed to be renewing the world, and that kind of unfashionableness is a part of the total cosmic renewal God is after.

1. What did you find new or especially thought provoking in this chapter's overview of the biblical story of Creation, the Fall, and redemption?

2. How would you explain the cultural mandate of Genesis 1:28 and the way in which it has been affected or not affected by the Fall?

3. Would you say that you've held what Tullian describes as an escapist view of redemption (i.e., the world is going to burn up, and believers should just look forward to going to heaven)? If so, where did you get that idea?

4. Read Romans 8:18–25. What evidences do you see around you of creation's "futility" and "bondage to corruption"?
5. How should grasping the big picture of Jesus's redeeming all things affect the way you live in this world?

Chapter 6. Redeemed to Renew

Evangelism is far from being the Christian's only responsibility; God wants us to renew the world in every way. We are to do nothing less than join him in bringing heaven into this world. We shouldn't expect to achieve such a transformation in a full sense until Jesus returns, but our efforts at cultural renewal still have eternal significance as we help to fulfill God's mission in our world.

1. Before you read this chapter, would you have said that evangelism is more important than cultural renewal? How has your thinking changed?
2. Read Revelation 21:1–22:5. What is it about this picture of a fully renewed world that makes your mouth water the most?
3. Give an example of the difference between persuasion and coercion when it comes to influencing society in a Godward direction.
4. What good and harm have you seen in Christian political activism?
5. What kinds of cultural transformation have you been a part of? How has it helped to serve the purposes of God?

Chapter 7. Presence of the Future

Most Christians have heard about the kingdom of God, but until we really understand what that kingdom is like, we won't understand our role in the world adequately. This kingdom is the rule and reign of God. Jesus inaugurated this kingdom when he came to earth; it continues today as we live under the leadership of the Lord; and one day, at the second coming of Jesus, it will be consummated and become a fully visible reality. It's by keeping this future consummation of the kingdom in mind that we know how to live unfashionably.

1. Is your citizenship in the kingdom of God something you think about frequently? occasionally? rarely? never?
2. As you read this chapter, what did you learn about the kingdom of God that you had never considered before?
3. What differences do you see between the continuation phase of the kingdom (the era in which we live) and the consummation phase (after Jesus's return)?
4. Read Isaiah 11:6–9. What qualities of the consummated kingdom does this passage give a glimpse of?
5. How does the knowledge that the Lord will return one day make a difference in your day-to-day life?

Chapter 8. Where in the World Are Christians?

We've heard that we are to be *in* the world but not *of* the world. But what does that mean? Well, it *doesn't* mean we are to try to keep ourselves separate and isolated from our culture. In fact, we are to engage our culture actively. Wherever we live, whatever we do, we are to reveal God's glory and reign right there. At the same time, of course, we can't let ourselves engage in the culture to the extent of participating in its sin. If we can effectively pull off this difficult in-but-not-of balancing act, the church can become a demonstration community, showing others what God wants to do in renewing the whole world.

1. Read John 17. What did Jesus request from his Father for his followers?
2. As chapter 8 describes it, what is the difference between *spiritual separation* and *spatial separation*? What is the difference between *contextualization* and *compromise*? What

are the differences among being culturally *removed*, culturally *relaxed*, and culturally *resistant*?

3. Would you say you have more of a problem with being legalistically separated from culture or with being sinfully entangled with culture? Why?

4. How can you glorify God in your work and among the people where you live?

5. How is your church serving as a demonstration community, as Tullian describes it? How is it falling short in that task?

Chapter 9. Unfashionably United

We live in a world where people tend to segregate themselves into comfortable affinity groups. And, sadly, the church is not much different. Christians, too, group themselves into "tribes" that make them feel safe instead of mixing with fellow believers of all descriptions. True, all Christians have a spiritual unity through our connection with Christ. But only as we are able to overcome our external divisions will we be effective in renewing the world and showing unbelievers what the love of God looks like. We need each other!

1. Read John 17 again—the same passage you read for chapter 8. This time look for what Jesus prayed in regard to Christian unity.

2. Would you say that you are a part of a Christian tribe? If so, what holds it together, and whom does it separate you from?

3. How do the unbelievers you know react to divisions within the Christian church?

4. What might a local church look like if it had no generational, ethnic, or similar barriers?

5. If a Christian wanted to pursue reconciliation and unity within the church, how might he go about it?

Chapter 10. Making the Difference Together

We, as Christians, are not expected to make a difference in the world on our own. We are to do it together. And therefore we need to become a connected people. As we do so, we'll show outsiders what God wants to do in the world: create real community based in him.

1. How has knowing Jesus changed you? How do you still need to be changed?

2. "There's no such thing as Christian individualism," says the author. "It's an oxymoron." What does he mean? And do you agree or disagree?

3. What causes individualism, and how can we overcome it?

4. If the church—collectively—were to do a better job of living as God asks us to, what do you think would be the reaction among unbelievers?

5. Read Ephesians 4. This passage includes the themes of unity and newness discussed in chapter 10 of this book. It also includes the put on/put off theme that will be revisited in the following chapters. For now, what kinds of changes in your life does this passage remind you that you need to make?

Chapter 11. A Truthful Community

One of the characteristics that an unfashionable, God-honoring church needs to acquire is truthfulness. Truth and trust go together—as we trust each other, we are willing to be honest with each other. One way we can establish this kind of trust with the world is to serve others simply for their own good, not because we're trying to get something from them. As we embody truthfulness, people will naturally be attracted by the God we worship; we won't have to sell him to them.

1. Read Acts 5:1–11. What does this story suggest about how lies affect a community? How do they affect God?

2. How would you describe the relationship between truth and trust? Which comes first—or do they have to exist simultaneously?

3. How can a church develop an atmosphere of greater trust?

4. How has your church tried to serve the wider community? Did it have a hidden agenda in doing so? What have been the results?

5. What can you, personally, do to raise the level of truthfulness within your church?

Chapter 12. An Angry Community

"The church is to be…an angry community," says Tullian. How about that! But he's not talking about the kind of self-centered anger that comes from personal slights. He's talking about God-centered anger that comes from hating what God hates: sin and evil, immorality and injustice. This kind of anger is not vindictive but rather is accompanied by grief over the suffering caused by human waywardness. And it starts with examining ourselves for any wrongdoing that deserves godly wrath.

1. What was your first reaction when you read the author's statement that the church is supposed to be an angry community? Why?

2. Give some examples of self-centered anger and God-centered anger, as Tullian defines these terms.

3. Read John 2:13–17. What makes this act qualify as God-centered anger?

4. What is wrong with anger without grief? What is wrong with grief without anger?

5. How, in your opinion, can today's church do a better job of living out God-centered anger?

Chapter 13. Putting Off Stealing

Another way in which the church is to be unfashionable is by reject-ing stealing in all forms. Some thefts of time, talents, and money are so common that they don't even get noticed—not fully using your gifts in a job and buying stuff you don't need are two examples. And then there's giving: "Christians ought to be known as the most gener-ous people on the face of this earth," says Tullian. This kind of gen-erosity comes from not just *understanding* but *sensing* God's own generosity toward us.

1. Which statement comes nearer the truth for you?
   a. I view my work as a necessary evil I face because I need to make money, and honestly, I can't wait until I have enough money to quit working.
   b. I view my work as a means of using the gifts God has given me to serve and improve the world.
2. Again, which statement comes nearer the truth for you?
   a. I spend all the money I've got (if not more, thanks to credit!) on the stuff and the experiences I crave.
   b. I buy what I need—that and little more—but more important, I try to maximize my giving to people who are more needy than I.
3. The author quotes Jim Elliot: "He is no fool who gives what he cannot keep to gain that which he cannot lose." What is it that you "cannot keep"? What is it that you "cannot lose"?
4. How has God been generous to you? How deeply would you say that you really *sense* this generosity?
5. Read Mark 12:41–44. What is the application here for you?

Chapter 14. Redemptive Words

Our temptation is to use words to manipulate people and get what we want; our challenge is to use words, instead, to encourage others, whether or not we get anything in return. Encouragement is redemptive speech. Speaking encouragement to unbelievers draws them toward God. Speaking encouragement to fellow believers reminds them of God within them.

1. How have you seen Christians use words in a way that unnecessarily pushed others away?
2. How have you seen Christians use words in a way that was encouraging, uplifting, or upbuilding to others?
3. Thinking of your local church, what grade would you give it for mutual encouragement: A, B, C, D, or F? How could it improve in this area?
4. How can you personally develop more godly speech habits?
5. Read 1 Thessalonians 5:14. Who are the "fainthearted" within your circle of acquaintances today? How can you encourage them?

Chapter 15. No Longer Clammed Up

Kindness is rare in our world; unkindness is the norm. And this prevalence of unkindness leads to people emotionally shutting down toward each other—it ruins relationships. Within the church, though, we ought to be relearning the art of kindness because of the marvelous kindness God has shown toward us. We ought to be warming up the cold world and reconnecting relationships with acts of kindness every day.

1. When was the last time you were stung by an act, a word, or a look of unkindness from somebody?
2. How have you seen somebody (maybe *you*) clamming up toward another person because of being hurt?
3. The author asks, "What would a community...look like where unkindness was nonexistent?" How would you answer that question?

4. Name one instance when the kindness of God moved you to be kind to another.
5. Read Luke 6:27–36. How does this passage say we ought to be kind? What does it say is our motivation for such kindness? What ideas does it give you about how you can show kindness today?

Chapter 16. Love, Not Lust

Ours is a sexually promiscuous society. And so, when the church stands against sex outside marriage, it can look like it's a spoilsport. Not so! Ungodly lust is the enemy of love, and love is what will fulfill people's deepest longings for relational intimacy. And so the church has to not just condemn immorality but, more important, to display love to unbelievers, unfashionable though it may be.

1. Tullian makes a case that sexual promiscuity is actually a sign of loneliness, not intimacy. Do you agree or disagree? Why?
2. Tullian also says that the bigger problem with sexual sin is not that it is dangerous but that it dehumanizes people. Again, do you agree or disagree, and why?
3. The prominent New Testament word for love—*agape*—implies self-sacrifice for another. In what ways does Jesus's life exemplify that kind of love?
4. Read 1 Corinthians 13. Taking each characteristic of love separately, how would you say you are doing at loving others in that way?
5. "We're to show our lonely world just how much more captivating and satisfying loving self-sacrifice is in comparison to sexual self-indulgence." How can we do that?

Chapter 17. Last Call

The world is not changed by big churches or by big ministries so much as by big Christians—people who have a large spiritual stature through faith, boldness, and determination. Such people refuse to get comfortable with the sinful patterns of the world. They don't care what others think about them; they care what *God* thinks about them. And when things get tough, they look to Christ, the trailblazer of unfashionability, to help them and bring them home.

1. Who are some big Christians you have known or read about? What made them big? What impact have they had on the world?

2. What would it take for you to become a big Christian? What scares you about that? What inspires you?

3. The phrase "against the world for the world" has appeared in the book many times, as it does in this final chapter. If you were to take it as a motto for your life, how would it change your interactions with others?

4. Read Hebrews 12:1–3. How can focusing on Jesus help you to fulfill God's call on your life?

5. Based on what you've read in this book, in what ways are you determined to become unfashionable?

ackn wledgments

I wrote this book because I had to. I don't mean that I was contractually obligated; I mean that it has been brewing in me for more than fourteen years, and if I hadn't gotten it out, I was going to explode. So I'd like to say thank you to many who have not only helped get this book out of me but in me as well.

First of all I'd like to thank my intellectual mentors. There are far too many to name them all. But fifteen thinkers in particular have shaped my understanding of the relationship between Christianity and culture: Os Guinness, John Seel, James Davison Hunter, Peter Berger, John Frame, David Wells, Stanley Hauerwas, Francis Schaeffer, Abraham Kuyper, William Willimon, Michael Horton, Tim Keller, Chuck Colson, Cornelius Plantinga, and, most recently, Andy Crouch. I am extremely grateful to God for these men and the way they have challenged me to become a man of "double listening."

To all my friends at Multnomah. Thank you for your interest in and support of this project from beginning to end.

To my editors, Thomas Womack and David Kopp. The two of you helped me start this book, and you helped me finish it. I thank God for your gifts. It's a great blessing to have editors who not only understand what you're trying to say but agree with you.

To my friends Brian Schutt and Justin Taylor. The two of you provided great editorial help along the way. Your suggestions made this a much stronger book.

To my New City Church family. It is a gift beyond measure that I get to be your pastor. In just five short years, you have helped establish an unfashionable community that is making a difference because it is different. Thank you. Thank God.

To Tim Keller for writing the foreword. I know how busy you are and how many demands are made on you, and yet you've always found time to talk with me, advise me, meet with me, and, in a thousand other ways, help me sort things out. So, Tim, thanks for all you do and for who you are. Preach on, brother—we're all listening!

To my children, Gabe, Nate, and Genna. I love you all so much. It is a pure joy to be your dad. Seriously! I can't wait to see how God is going to use each of you as you set your hearts and minds to living against the world for the world.

To my wife, Kim. This book is dedicated to you. Your willingness to follow my unfashionable lead and to be unfashionable with me keeps me pressing on and straining forward. Till death do us part!

n●tes

Chapter 2: A World Without Windows

1. Peter L. Berger and Richard Neuhaus, eds., *Against the World for the World: The Hartford Appeal and the Future of American Religion* (New York: Seabury Press, 1976).

2. Os Guinness, *The Gravedigger File: Papers on the Subversion of the Modern Church* (Downers Grove, IL: InterVarsity Press, 1983), 56.

3. Os Guinness, *Dining with the Devil: The Megachurch Movement Flirts with Modernity* (Grand Rapids: Baker, 1993), 48.

4. Os Guinness, *Long Journey Home: A Guide to Your Search for the Meaning of Life* (New York: Doubleday, 2001), 16.

5. Gene Edward Veith Jr., *Postmodern Times: A Christian Guide to Contemporary Thought and Culture* (Wheaton, IL: Crossway, 1994), 227.

6. Ed Stetzer, quoted in Audrey Barrick, "Unchurched Prefer Cathedrals over Contemporary Church Buildings," *Christian Post,* April 7, 2008, www.christianpost.com/article/20080407/unchurched-prefer-cathedrals-over-contemporary-church-buildings.htm.

7. Os Guinness, *The Devil's Gauntlet: The Church and the Challenge of Society* (Downers Grove, IL: InterVarsity Press, 1989), 30.

8. Julie R. Neidlinger, "Why I Walked Out of Church," Loneprairie.net, www.loneprairie.net/lp_studies/2008/08/why-i-walked-out-of-church.htm.

9. Mickey McLean, "Why She Walked Out of Church," *World,* August 6, 2008, online.worldmag.com/2008/08/06/why-she-walked-out-of-church/.

10. Lauren Winner, "Gen X Revisited: A Return to Tradition?" *Christian Century,* November 8, 2000, 1147.

Chapter 3: Seduced by Cool

1. Arthur Bennett, *The Valley of Vision* (Carlisle, PA: Banner of Truth, 1975), xxiv.
2. C. S. Lewis, *The Great Divorce* (New York: HarperCollins, 2001), 119.
3. Timothy Keller, *The Reason for God: Belief in an Age of Skepticism* (New York: Dutton, 2008), 196.
4. C. S. Lewis, *The Screwtape Letters* (New York: HarperCollins, 2001), 135.
5. Flannery O'Connor, *The Habit of Being: Letters,* ed. Sally Fitzgerald (New York: Vintage Books, 1980), 90.
6. Iain H. Murray, *Evangelicalism Divided: A Record of Crucial Change in the Years 1950–2000* (Carlisle, PA: Banner of Truth, 2000), 149.
7. David F. Wells, *God in the Wasteland: The Reality of Truth in a World of Fading Dreams* (Grand Rapids: Eerdmans, 1994), 36.

Chapter 4: An Unfashionable Standard

1. Luke Timothy Johnson, quoted in Richard John Neuhaus, "The Future of Sex and Marriage," *First Things,* January 4, 2008, www.firstthings.com/onthesquare/?p=943.
2. Michael Horton, "Are Churches Secularizing America?" *Modern Reformation,* March-April 2008, www.modernreformation.org/default.php?page=articledisplay&var1=ArtRead&var2=917&var3=issuedisplay&var4=IssRead&var5=98.
3. Chuck Colson, quoted in T. M. Moore, *Culture Matters: A Call for Consensus on Christian Cultural Engagement* (Grand Rapids: Brazos, 2007), 117.
4. Francis A. Schaeffer, *A Christian Manifesto* (Wheaton, IL: Crossway, 1982), 20.
5. J. I. Packer, *God's Plans for You* (Wheaton, IL: Good News, 2001), 20.
6. J. I. Packer, *Truth and Power: The Place of Scripture in the Christian Life* (Downers Grove, IL: InterVarsity Press, 1999), 156.
7. Packer, *Truth and Power,* 165.

Chapter 5: The Purpose-Driven Death

1. Jeff Purswell, "How to Love the World," in *Worldliness: Resisting the Seduction of a Fallen World,* ed. C. J. Mahaney (Wheaton, IL: Crossway, 2008), 143.

2. Nancy Pearcey, *Total Truth: Liberating Christianity from Its Cultural Captivity* (Wheaton, IL: Crossway, 2004), 47.

3. John Seel, "It's the Culture, Stupid: Reflections on the Challenge of Cultural Influence."

4. Vern Poythress, "The Reversal of the Curse," *Tabletalk,* March 2004, 8.

5. Michael E. Wittmer, *Heaven Is a Place on Earth: Why Everything You Do Matters to God* (Grand Rapids: Zondervan, 2004), 187.

6. John Calvin, *Institutes of the Christian Religion,* ed. John T. McNeill, trans. Ford Lewis Battles (Philadelphia: Westminster, 1960), 3.1.1.

7. Note on 2 Peter 3:10 in the *ESV Study Bible* (Wheaton, IL: Crossway, 2008), 2422–23. This note is heavily influenced by Douglas J. Moo, "Nature in the New Creation: New Testament Eschatology and the Environment," *Journal of the Evangelical Theological Society* 49 (2006): 449–88.

8. Note on 2 Peter 3:10 in the *ESV Study Bible* (Wheaton, IL: Crossway, 2008), 2422–23.

9. Randy Alcorn, *Heaven for Kids* (Carol Stream, IL: Tyndale, 2006), 53.

10. Cornelius Plantinga, *Engaging God's World: A Christian Vision of Faith, Learning, and Living* (Grand Rapids: Eerdmans, 2002), 139.

Chapter 6: Redeemed to Renew

1. Rick McKinley, *This Beautiful Mess* (Sisters, OR: Multnomah, 2006), 79.

2. K. Scott Oliphint and Sinclair B. Ferguson, *If I Should Die Before I Wake: What's Beyond This Life?* (Fearn, Scotland: Christian Focus, 2004), 71.

3. John Stott, *The Contemporary Christian: Applying God's Word to Today's World* (Leicester, England: InterVarsity Press, 1992), 85.

4. John Piper, *The Pleasures of God: Meditations on God's Delight in Being God* (Portland, OR: Multnomah, 1990), 24.

5. John M. Frame, *The Doctrine of the Christian Life* (Phillipsburg, NJ: P&R Publishing, 2008), 862.

6. Michael E. Wittmer, *Heaven Is a Place on Earth: Why Everything You Do Matters to God* (Grand Rapids: Zondervan, 2004), 188.

7. This distinction has helped me disconnect the link often made (mistakenly) between a transformational view of culture and a Christian reconstructionist (or theonomist) view—the idea that it's the Christian's responsibility to "reconstruct" our world by applying the case laws of Old Testament Israel. Transformationalists endorse persuasion. Christian reconstuctionists endorse coercion.

8. Ethelwyn Wetherald, quoted in John Seel and Os Guinness, eds., *No God but God* (Chicago: Moody Press, 1992), 79.

9. Frame, *The Doctrine of the Christian Life,* 874.

10. Vern S. Poythress, "A 'Day of Small Things,'" *World,* March 8, 2008, www.worldmag.com/articles/13793.

11. Cal Thomas, "Religious Right, R.I.P.," *Jewish World Review,* November 6, 2008, www.jewishworldreview.com/cols/thomas110608.php3.

12. Richard John Neuhaus, "Christ Without Culture, Etc.," *First Things,* April 2007, www.firstthings.com/article.php3?id_article=5460.

Chapter 7: Presence of the Future

1. John Murray, *Redemption Accomplished and Applied* (Grand Rapids: Eerdmans, 1955), 145.

2. Sinclair B. Ferguson, *The Sermon on the Mount* (Carlisle, PA: Banner of Truth, 1987), 3.

3. George Eldon Ladd, *The Gospel of the Kingdom: Scriptural Studies in the Kingdom of God* (Grand Rapids: Eerdmans, 1959), 22.

4. I'm indebted to my former professor Richard L. Pratt Jr., who chairs the Old Testament department at Reformed Theological Seminary in Orlando, Florida, for first introducing me to this terminology and the idea that the kingdom of God unfolds in three stages.

5. Richard L. Pratt Jr., *He Gave Us Stories: The Bible Student's Guide to Interpreting Old Testament Narratives* (Phillipsburg, NJ: P&R Publishing, 1990), 353.

6. Maurice Roberts, *Great God of Wonders* (Edinburgh: Banner of Truth, 2003), 51.

Chapter 8: Where in the World Are Christians?

1. Dick Staub, *Too Christian, Too Pagan: How to Love the World Without Falling for It* (Grand Rapids: Zondervan, 2000), back cover.

2. Staub, *Too Christian, Too Pagan,* 16.

3. Andy Crouch, *Culture Making: Rediscovering Our Creative Calling* (Downers Grove, IL: InterVarsity Press, 2008), 69.

4. John Frame, *The Doctrine of the Christian Life* (Phillipsburg, NJ: P&R Publishing, 2008), 874.

5. C. S. Lewis, quoted in Don E. Eberly, *Restoring the Good Society: A New Vision for Politics and Culture* (Grand Rapids: Baker, 1994), 80.

6. Chuck Colson and Ellen Vaughn, *Being the Body* (Nashville: W Publishing, 2003), 371.

7. Edith Schaeffer, quoted in Colin Duriez, *Francis Schaeffer: An Authentic Life* (Wheaton, IL: Crossway, 2008), 163.

8. Marcia Segelstein, "Calling Christian Rebels," *BreakPoint,* May 24, 2007, www.breakpoint.org/listingarticle.asp?ID=6520.

9. Mike Metzger, *Fine-Tuning Tensions Within Culture: The Art of Being Salt and Light* (Suwannee, GA: Relevate, 2007), 4.

Chapter 9: Unfashionably United

1. C. S. Lewis, *The Four Loves* (New York: Harcourt, Brace, 1960), 52.

2. Todd Pruitt, e-mail message to the author, July 12, 2008.

3. "The Heidelberg Catechism," Christian Reformed Church, www
   .crcna.org/pages/heidelberg_commandments.cfm.
4. *Book of Common Prayers* (New York: HarperOne, 1983), 818.
5. Reggie Kidd, "Herodotus—Mutual Defenestration Means Self Annihilation," *With One Voice,* September 3, 2007, http://reggiekidd.com/
   RK/2007/09/03/favorite-quotes-herodotus-mutual-defenestration-
   means-self-annihilation/.

Chapter 10: Making the Difference Together
1. C. S. Lewis, *Mere Christianity* (New York: HarperCollins, 2001), 216.

Chapter 11: A Truthful Community
1. Preston Jones, "How to Serve Time," *Christianity Today,* April 2001,
   www.ctlibrary.com/ct/2001/april2/2.50.html.
2. Jerry Bridges, *Respectable Sins: Confronting the Sins We Tolerate* (Colorado Springs, CO: NavPress, 2007), 172–73.

Chapter 12: An Angry Community
1. John R. W. Stott, *The Message of Ephesians* (Downers Grove, IL:
   InterVarsity Press, 1979), 186.

Chapter 13: Putting Off Stealing
1. "Credit Card Debt Statistics," Money-Zine.com, www.money-zine
   .com/financial-planning/debt-consolidation/credit-card-debt-statistics.

Chapter 14: Redemptive Words
1. John R. W. Stott, *The Message of Ephesians* (Downers Grove, IL:
   InterVarsity Press, 1979), 188.
2. John Piper, "An Invitation to an Unusual Conference," desiringGod,
   July 30, 2008, www.desiringgod.org/ResourceLibrary/TasteAndSee/
   ByDate/2008/3089/.
3. David F. Wells, *God in the Wasteland: The Reality of Truth in a World
   of Fading Dreams* (Grand Rapids: Eerdmans, 1994), 11.

Chapter 16: Love, Not Lust

1. Trevin Wax, *Subversive Allegiance* (Wheaton, IL: Crossway, forthcoming).
2. Andy Crouch, "The Pleasures and Perils of Fermentation," *Culture Making*, www.culture-making.com/articles/pleasures_and_perils_of_fermentation.
3. John Seel, "Scaring the Sex out of You," unpublished paper.
4. C. S. Lewis, *The Four Loves* (New York: Harcourt, Brace, 1960), 121.
5. John Piper, *The Legacy of Sovereign Joy: God's Triumphant Grace in the Lives of Augustine, Luther, and Calvin* (Wheaton, IL: Good News, 2000), 48, 51.
6. Piper, *Legacy of Sovereign Joy,* 53.

Chapter 17: Last Call

1. John Foxe, *Foxe's Christian Martyrs of the World* (Uhrichsville, OH: Barbour, 1989), 11–12.
2. E. M. Bounds, *The Complete Works of E. M Bounds on Prayer* (Grand Rapids: Baker, 1990), 447.
3. David Wells, *God in the Wasteland: The Reality of Truth in a World of Fading Dreams* (Grand Rapids: Eerdmans, 1994), 30.
4. Wells, *God in the Wasteland,* 214–15.
5. Sinclair B. Ferguson, *Grow in Grace* (Carlisle, PA: Banner of Truth, 1989), 10.

index

ab●ut the author

WILLIAM GRAHAM TULLIAN TCHIVIDJIAN (pronounced *cha-vi-jin*) is a Florida native, the founding pastor of New City Church just outside of Fort Lauderdale, Florida, a visiting professor of theology at Reformed Theological Seminary, and a grandson of Billy and Ruth Graham. A graduate of Columbia International University (in philosophy) and Reformed Theological Seminary in Orlando, Tullian is the author of *The Kingdom of God: A Primer on the Christian Life* and *Do I Know God? Finding Certainty in Life's Most Important Relationship*. The author of numerous articles, Tullian is a contributing editor to *Leadership Journal*. Tullian speaks at conferences throughout the United States, and his sermons are broadcast daily on the radio program *Godward Living*.

When he is not reading, studying, preaching, or writing, he enjoys being with people and relaxing with his wife, Kim, and their three kids, Gabe, Nate, and Genna. Tullian loves going to the beach, exercising, and—when he has time—surfing.

Some of Tullian's favorite authors include C. S. Lewis, John Stott, Charles Colson, J. I. Packer, Jonathan Edwards, and G. K. Chesterton. He also happens to be a music buff who likes listening to basically every kind of music except country.

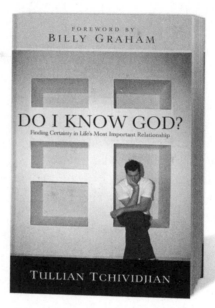